ONE
Unforgettable
JOURNEY

Dan Stallings

K.B. Lacoste

This work is based on true events. However, names of people or places may have been changed to protect those involved.

Proofreading by SuperCopyEditors.com

Printed in the United States of America
First Printing, 2012
ISBN: 1477600329
ISBN-13: 978-1477600320

This book is dedicated to the many rescue groups who work tirelessly to help dogs in unfortunate situations find better, happier, healthier lives and the love they truly deserve.

Extraordinary Praise for
One Unforgettable Journey

"Every reputable breeder can relate to the panic when 'one of his/hers' is unaccounted for. Every rescue person can tell a dozen horror stories of abuse and neglect. Every rescue volunteer can tell stories of happy endings. But only Dan can tell Maverick's story – his story will leave a paw print on your heart."

–Dr. Dana Massey, Breeder/Owner Win'Weim Weimaraners and AKC Judge

"It seems like you can't look ten feet these days without running into someone's memoir about their dog. They're everywhere, and they all kind of blend into one story after a while – except Dan and Maverick. Their story has something for everyone, whether you are a dog fancy expert, rescue advocate, or just someone who is moved by the power of one man's unwavering belief inside this neglected creature he found on Craigslist was the heart of a champion. It's a story you would find hard to believe if it were a work of fiction because it's just such an unbelievable trajectory. Way to go Mav!"

-Jessica Vogelsang, DVM, author and owner Pawcurious Media

"As many dog books and stories of rescue that I've encountered over the years, this one is something unlike anything that I've ever heard. Having had the privilege to meet Dan and Maverick in person, I can testify that the love that emanates between the two of them is incredibly powerful, as is the bond that they have forged. One Unforgettable Journey is the story of a man with a heart of gold, and a dog with the heart of a champion."

-Dr. Katy Nelson - Veterinarian, Host of The Pet Show with Dr. Katy on Washington DC's News Channel 8, WTOP's "Dr. Pawz," and host of Pawsitive Talk on HealthyLife.Net

"It's not very often that one has the opportunity to peer into a world that is beyond ourselves. Animal rescues, dog shows and life choices are just a handful to mention. But One Unforgettable Journey encompasses more than that. With a fire-side chat nostalgia, Dan and Kristine lay out a light yet heartwarming tale of a Maverick: a dog who truly begets his name. Whether a pet owner, fancier or someone who just appreciates the bonds we have with our four legged friends, this book carries the tones of how every rescue can and often is the Best in our hearts."

-Xavier A. Santiago, International Actor, On-Air Host, Animal Planet's Groomer Has It Judge, Producer, Breeder and Professional Handler

Acknowledgements

There are so many people who were all a part of Maverick's recovery and triumph, but first and foremost I would like to thank my best friends who also happen to be my parents. My dad from whom I inherited the dog person genes and my mom for all her patience and wisdom with running my business which is what allows me to help all these beautiful gray dogs in my rescue.

The people without whom I never would have even known about Maverick: Chris and Dianne Gordonn. Thank you for your diligence and generous hearts.

Jan Lowe, Maverick's breeder who was so helpful in detailing Mav's past and mentoring me every step of the way.

Thanks to my friend Sarah for helping me learn the ropes as I stumbled through most of the early dog shows not even knowing what my boy had accomplished.

Darlene Bergen who's gentle guidance reintroduced Mav to the show world in a way he would enjoy and eventually win.

The one person who took Mav to a whole new level and made him shine in the brightest of spotlights was his handler, Rusty Howard. He and his assistants, Jessie Sheaves and Brittany Dunas handled Mav brilliantly and got the very best out of him. I was very fortunate to have Rusty at his side in the ring and without the results of all his hard work, this journey wouldn't be nearly as unforgettable.

The entire Bacon family: Steve, Cindy, Taylor and Abbey for putting up with Mav and I while at his first major in Ohio and for showing him off to all their friends like he was already a champion. For going out of your way to watch him show, earn his Grand Champion title and for driving 9 hours just to watch him show on the green carpet of the Garden.

I would be remiss if I didn't let Vicki Seiler with Eukanuba know how much I appreciate her setting up the adverts featuring Mav so prominently. Who would've thought the skinny weim I took in would one day be featured in several Eukanuba dog food ads? Thank you for all the kind words.

There is one special fan of Mav's I have to thank for all her support and cheering. Mav's biggest fan from Canada: Darlene Howard-Perry.

One of the things that made the New York show so special was all the phone calls I got the weekend before the show.

Thank you to the reporter who called me from a family trip in England to get Mav's story and later turned out to be my co-author, Kristine Lacoste.

Thanks to Dr. Jessica Vogelsang, whose reaction to Mav and how people were drawn to him led her to do an additional piece about him on her blog aside from the one she was originally commissioned to do by Eukanuba.

I would also like to thank Dan Harris of ABC news for taking such an interest in Mav's story and getting it on the ABC World News Tonight. Your piece introduced the world to Maverick and his story. So many people who saw that have reached out to me and told me how wonderful it was.

Thank you to all of the AKC judges who awarded this deserving dog. He will always be my first Champion, Grand Champion and my Best in Show!

ONE
UNFORGETTABLE
JOURNEY

ONE

The small, light blue sedan turned into the driveway and slowly crept closer to the building. After coming to a stop, the engine quieted and the driver's door opened almost immediately. Dan put on his best smile and walked toward the man without any idea of the horror he was about to see.

He introduced himself and thanked the visitor for making the journey to his shop until the other car doors opened. The wife emerged from the passenger door, but Dan's focus was on the rear door.

A child exited the vehicle and turned to pull on a leash. The outline of a slender dog sitting in the back seat was illuminated by the sunshine filtering through the rear window of the car. The shadow made its way toward the door and slowly jumped down onto the concrete. For a brief moment he was out of view, and the child soon came around the car holding the leash.

Dan arched his neck to look over and get a glimpse of the dog. The advertisement described the Weimaraner as a competitive show dog. Dan didn't know much about dog shows, but he found it odd that the dog was listed.

Dog shows were quite a change in direction, although Dan was no stranger to change. He was working in medical device sales when he acquired his first Weimaraner through a course of events that seemed destined to occur. He was on his way to work when his car ran over roofing nails on the highway, puncturing holes in two tires. The car was towed to a local tire company but the tires he needed were not in stock. They were ordered from across town but would take two hours to arrive.

While Dan was waiting for the tires to arrive, he noticed a pet store in the shopping center nearby. He figured he could pass the time by picking out a toy for his girlfriend's dog and started walking toward the entrance.

As Dan approached, a little puppy came bounding toward him and started running in circles around him wrapping the leash around his legs. The puppy was being walked by one of the store employees, who apologized for the sudden meeting, though Dan didn't mind. The puppy was beautiful and he told her so as he walked into the store.

"Can you believe someone abandoned her?" she said.

"You're kidding," he replied.

"Nope. A woman came to the vet counter and asked us to hold the leash for her while she got something out of her car and never came back," she explained.

Dan was stunned. "That's so sad. I hope you guys find her a permanent home."

He wished them luck and walked down the aisle to look for dog toys. He found a suitable toy and completed his purchase before heading back to check on his car. A few hours later the new tires were installed. It was too late in the day to drive to work so he headed home.

Dan thought about the little puppy often during his two-hour drive home. He couldn't get her out of his head, so as soon as he arrived home he called the pet store to check on her availability. There were four people signed up to adopt her, and they said they would call him if the first four people didn't work out.

Over the next two weeks Dan called and checked on the puppy. The list of four dropped to two then dwindled to one remaining person, but he had no choice but to wait for the last person to decline the adoption. He finally got the call he was waiting for and drove two hours to the pet store to pick up his new puppy. He named her Lexi and took her home.

Dan traveled constantly for work and this made time with Lexi difficult over the next few months. He didn't like the idea of leaving her crated and alone all day, so he adopted another Weimaraner he named Luger to keep her company.

Leaving the dogs every day became increasingly difficult, and one day Dan decided to take them along when he traveled. He started finding various day care centers near his destination to drop the dogs off during the day while he worked. After work he would pick them up for the night and return them the next day until it was time to return home.

These road trips took him and the dogs to several states, and before long he had a glove compartment full of pamphlets for pet boarders and play places for his two companions.

The travel became tedious, the hours were long, and he found himself wanting to spend more time with the dogs. He figured there had to be a better way to spend time with his dogs instead of traveling all the time, so he decided to enroll in a school to become a certified trainer. He quit his job and decided to open his own canine facility. Finding a place on the road that would offer multiple services was difficult, so he was determined that his shop would do it all: boarding, grooming, training, behavior modification, and take in any Weimaraner rescues that needed help.

Luckily he was able to find a property nearby so he would never have to be far from the dogs. It started out small but quickly turned into a busy place. Soon there were dogs everywhere; the outdoor areas and diving dock quickly became favorites, as well as the comfortable sofas placed throughout the lobby and shop. It looked like a dog's paradise, and Dan was happy.

Dogs started coming in, and some days there would be more than 100 daily clients at a time. Rescues also increased, and other Weimaraner rescue groups started sending their worst cases to Dan's shop. Some of the rescues had behavioral issues or needed training, and others were never socialized. Those dogs usually ended up as permanent residents, and before he knew it Dan had 17 dogs he kept as his own pets. After socializing and rehabilitating a dog, Dan would always try to find a job or purpose that the dog enjoyed.

Some of his dogs loved obedience trials, while others adored dock diving. They would run at full speed down the wooden dock and leap high into the air before landing in the water, only to swim out and head back to the dock again. There was a dock for diving at the shop, and employees would train any dog that showed interest. Dan started taking them to dock diving competitions, and the dogs loved not only the socialization but also getting to spend the day running and swimming.

Dan had never given much thought to dog shows, but a friend called him when he noticed a Weimaraner listed for sale in an online newspaper. Dan was always unsettled when one of these dogs was listed without a reason given; if cared for properly, Weimaraners are goofy and affectionate dogs that make such great pets that no one would want to give them up. He would usually contact the owners and ask them to sign the dog over to the rescue so the dog would be cared for properly.

The listing did say that it was a show dog, and since Dan didn't really know much about shows, he didn't give it much thought. He was interested in the idea of meeting a dog groomed for this purpose and figured he'd learn a thing or two about these competitions that were so foreign to him at the time.

Dan's excitement turned to shock when the dog came around the front of the car. He was horrified at what he saw. Before him stood a dog so thin his every bone was visible. He slowly walked on painfully overgrown nails. He had a pressure sore on his chest, an infected wound on his nose, and his tail and paws were chewed until they were raw. The child dragged him to the front of the car, and when the dog wouldn't sit, the child hit him on his back and pushed his rear down on the concrete.

When Dan took a step toward him, the dog lowered his head. Dan knew that wasn't normal and wondered what had been done to this poor guy to be in such a state of neglect and fear.

"This is a show dog?"

The man replied, "Yeah, he's got some points under his belt. Pay no mind to how he looks; he's just a picky eater and doesn't eat much."

His wife chimed in, "If he knew how to behave around kids properly he wouldn't have to be crated all day. I can't take much more of him."

Weimaraners are not the kind of dogs that take to excessive crating well, and Dan knew this from experience. His horror had turned to sadness, and he knew he had to get the dog out of that situation. If the dog lost any more weight, he might get really sick – or worse, be dropped off at a shelter or vet and be neutered. Weimaraners typically don't handle shelter environments well. They feel isolated, lonely, and some simply shut down and refuse to eat. Those are the ones usually classified as priority pickups when he gets a notification sent in to the rescue. If they refuse to eat or respond from shutting down, they are more likely to be considered unsuitable for adoption and euthanized. Dan imagined this transpiring and knew he couldn't let the dog leave today.

TWO

Dan forgot all about the dog shows and was intent on making sure this dog got the help it needed.

"Did you want to sign him over to the rescue so we can take care of him?" Dan asked.

"Sign him over? I paid for this dog and want some of my money out of him," the man replied. "I'm not just going to sign him over."

Dan was surprised and asked him, "Can't you see he needs help? Look at his bones sticking out. This dog looks sick and needs immediate care. I've taken in strays that look better than him."

The owner was intent on recouping the money he had paid the breeder.

"He's just a picky eater. Maybe you can find something he likes. Look, we can negotiate on price, but I'm not going to just give him away."

Dan decided he didn't care what it would cost; there was no way the dog was leaving with those people.

They agreed on a price, and Dan returned to his office to get his checkbook. He placed an urgent call to his vet's office explaining the dog's condition and told them he would be on his way in a few minutes. He was glad they were able to see him so soon; if not, he would have headed to the animal hospital.

He glanced out the window to make sure the family was still there as he quickly wrote the check.

Dan went back outside to make the exchange, and the owner said he would forward the breed paperwork in about a week. The dog cowered again when approached, and Dan spoke low and gently as he guided him away from the car by his leash.

The family got back in the car, and as they were about to leave, Dan asked, "Wait, what's his name?"

"Maverick," the man said before backing out of the driveway and disappearing.

"Maverick, eh?" Dan said to the dog as he looked down at him. "Well Maverick, let's go get you some help."

Dan picked him up and put him in his vehicle to head to the vet's office. He was surprised and disgusted at how light the dog was, and he wondered what other ailments the dog was suffering from. Maverick sat in the rear of the sport utility vehicle, and after making sure he was secure, Dan closed the rear door and got in his seat to drive to the vet.

Dan pulled into the parking lot and headed in with Maverick. The dog was skittish and unsure of his surroundings as he was led into the vet's office. He kept his head down and hid behind Dan's legs while he checked in at the front desk. A quick glance around the waiting room revealed a few people already waiting, but the receptionist said the wait would not be long.

Dan found an empty chair and led Maverick over by his lead to sit in front of him. His tail wasn't wagging and he looked petrified. Dan looked up and met the eyes of a man sitting across from him. The man looked down at Maverick and back at Dan before making a disgusted face and looking away.

"I don't treat dogs like this!" Dan wanted to yell across the room. He felt humiliated and hung his head down while looking at Maverick. He was preparing himself for the worst and dreaded the heartworm test. Most neglected dogs do not receive proper prevention or treatment for heartworms, and this can be a death sentence. Dogs healthy enough to receive treatment face months of medication and must be kept calm, mostly by crating, to prevent serious complications that can be deadly. Maverick had just been removed from a situation where he was excessively crated and he suffered greatly because of it. If he was positive for heartworms, Dan feared for the dog's mental state if he faced crating again.

Dan's name was finally called, and he headed into the examination room. He thanked the vet tech for seeing him so soon and explained his new companion.

She placed Maverick on top of the table in the center of the room. The tech winced when she looked at Maverick. The dog was in obvious discomfort and painfully thin. She also noticed the overgrown nails the dog was walking on and figured she would start by clipping those.

She grabbed the clippers and reached for a paw, but Maverick pulled back. She tried again and he backed up to the end of the table. He was calm up to this point but began flipping out when she tried to extend his paw. He was frightened and crouched into a ball on the corner of the examination table.

Dan suggested they move him to the floor and try again. As soon as Maverick's paws hit the floor he backed into a corner.

"Are you sure you want to continue?" she asked Dan.

"Yes," he replied, "there is no way he's walking on those anymore. They have to be clipped."

"All right."

A moment later Dan heard the door open and saw the manager looking in. She looked at the situation on the floor and then to Dan, who replied, "Hi! Here's my new show dog!"

The manager tilted her head to the side in amusement and walked in laughing.

"You guys look like you could use some help."

It took all three of them to restrain and clip Maverick's nails. Dan and the two vet techs worked quickly but were still on the floor when the vet walked in.

The vet asked what was happening.

"This guy doesn't want his nails clipped," the vet tech replied. "Almost there… and done."

The vet tech went to the table to set the clippers down and prepared materials to collect test samples. Dan returned Maverick to the table for the vet to examine him.

"Got another rescue, eh Dan?"

Dan chuckled. "He was listed as a show dog," he said, "but as you can see, he's a rescue from a very bad situation."

The vet looked at the dog and back to Dan with a puzzled look. "This is a show dog? He looks like one of your rescues, you're right."

"I didn't know what to expect with a show dog, but no dog should look like this."

"Agreed."

He started examining Maverick and making notes. The list was long: pressure sores, skin infections, self-mutilation wounds, muscle atrophy, paws and tail sore and raw, bones protruding from lack of food, and muscle waste. Tests would be run to rule out any serious conditions or infections. He drew a few vials of blood and took a fecal sample to run tests for heartworms and parasites.

"Let me go run these tests in our lab down the hall, and I'll be back with you as soon as I can," the vet said before gathering the tubes and paperwork.

"Okay, thanks," Dan replied and tried to comfort Maverick.

The vet and the techs left the room. Dan looked over Maverick's nails and hoped the trim would help him with walking and reduce his discomfort. The vet returned a short time later with papers in hand.

"Well, I've got good news and bad news. The good news is he doesn't have any parasites or heartworms. The bad news is I can't find a medical reason for his condition. That means it's down to neglect."

Dan suspected this all along, but he was relieved to hear nothing serious seemed to be ailing Maverick.

"You got him just in time, Dan. He'll need to get his weight up and rebuild muscle, and I'll give you something to put on his sores. I'd also like to start him on antibiotics, but just for a couple of weeks as a precaution."

He handed Dan a bottle of pills, a tube of ointment, and Vitamin E.

"The antibiotics need to be taken with food over the next two weeks. The ointment and Vitamin E should last you a month," he instructed. "You're all set. Come back in if anything changes."

They shook hands and left the room. The vet guided Dan to the front desk and patted Maverick on the head. "See you in a few weeks, little buddy."

As Dan walked back to the truck, he noticed Maverick didn't have a collar or tag around his neck. That would be his next stop before heading back to the shop. Dan had collars at the shop but didn't have a tag machine.

He loaded Maverick into the rear area of the sport utility vehicle and remembered that the local pet store had a tag machine by its entrance. He headed there and had a tag engraved with Maverick's name and contact information.

The day was coming to an end and there were just a few things left to do at the shop. Dan walked Maverick through the lobby and grabbed a collar before heading into his office. He affixed the collar and closed the gate to the room. The gate was only waist-high and could be seen through, so it shouldn't feel too restrictive on the dog. Dan went to quickly wrap up his remaining tasks so he could return his attention to Maverick.

THREE

Dan was finished at the shop in an hour, and he headed home with Maverick in tow. Once inside he showed Maverick to an area where he could lie down. Dan went to the kitchen to prepare a dish with food and the crushed antibiotics. He returned to Maverick and placed the dish at his paws. The dog looked at the food then back to Dan without touching the dish. Dan was confused and thought Maverick had to have been hungry by now. Dan pushed the dish closer, but the dog still wouldn't eat.

"Not your brand, eh?"

Dan headed back to the kitchen to try a different brand of food. He filled another dish and returned with his offering. He moved the first dish and placed the new one down in front of Maverick. The dog looked at the dish and back at Dan again.

Dan stood there puzzled and told him, "You can't get better if you don't eat." Dan didn't know the specific circumstances of Maverick's everyday care and feeding, and he wondered if perhaps he preferred to eat when alone. So Dan left another dish with water and decided to call it a night. He would check back in the morning and hope that one of the two dishes would be empty.

Morning came quickly, and Dan's first thought was of Maverick. He showered and dressed and went to check on him. Maverick's head lifted from the pillow when Dan walked in. Sadly, the two dishes of food were still sitting there untouched. Dan felt deflated but not defeated. He had at least nine other brands of dog food at his shop, and Maverick was sure to like one of them.

He grabbed the ointment and starting putting it on Maverick's nose. Before he could finish spreading it around it was being licked off. He tried again and off it went.

"How are you supposed to get better if you don't leave this on?"

Dan shook his head as Maverick kept licking his nose. The dog stopped and looked up at him with sad eyes.

"Awe, come on. Don't look at me like that. You know I have to do this."

Dan added a little more ointment to his nose and other sores. To stop the ointment from being licked off he added tea tree oil on the top of his paws and tail to try to keep it in place. They had to leave for the shop and headed in to start the day. Dan went through his morning routine quickly so he could turn his attention to Maverick.

Perusing the shelves, he grabbed a high-protein food that the other dogs loved. It usually disappeared in minutes when offered, so this one was sure to do the trick. Maverick was in his office again today, and Dan headed in with the new food.

It was a repeat of last night; Maverick just looked at the dish and back up at him. Dan shook his head and removed the dish. He returned to the shelves to try another type of food. And another. And another. Dan tried every brand and type of food he had in the shop, and Maverick refused every single one. The rest of the day and night was the same as the first. He was getting worried because if Maverick kept refusing food, that also meant he wasn't getting any antibiotics into his system. He applied the ointment at night, hoping some of it would stay before trying again in the morning.

Both dishes were still full when Dan woke. This was the second day Maverick didn't eat, and he was too underweight to skip meals. Dan applied the ointment again and wondered what kind of food he should try next.

Dan went into the shop as usual with Maverick, and he hoped today would be more successful. Maverick went back in his office while Dan searched the shelves for more ideas. He reached for the treats in a last-ditch effort to get him to eat something. He went back into the office and placed a treat by his paws with the same result: Nothing.

Dan sat down in front of Maverick and rubbed his head.

"You have to eat something."

He picked up the treat and held it in his hand as he sat there trying to think of other ways to get him to eat. He felt something cold and wet touch his hand, and he looked down to find Maverick taking the treat out of his hand.

"Ah, so hand fed treats will work. That's a start!"

Dan was excited to find something—anything—that Maverick would eat. Treats were not ideal as a source of food, but they might lead the way for more meals. Dan went back to the front of the shop and returned to his office armed with two bags of treats. He sat there and hand fed Maverick until the dog didn't want any more and laid his head down.

Dan returned to the office a few times that day to offer treats, apply the ointment the vet had provided, and take Maverick for walks. He was interested and friendly with every dog that would approach him. Most of the dogs would lie on the sofas in the shop, but Maverick preferred the rug by the door. He was still a little skittish and wary of his surroundings. He only seemed to lower his head when people approached him or extended an arm to touch him. Dan hoped this would get better with time, but for now the focus was on getting the dog's health and diet to better levels.

Later that night Dan tried canned dog food to no avail. He continued hand feeding treats for the night and tried to think of other foods he hadn't tried yet. Maverick was getting used to the ointment and wasn't licking it off, so at least that was working out. Dan was applying it twice a day now, but he still had to find a solution for the food.

The next day he went back to the store and searched the dog food aisle for ideas. There was a raw kibble he hadn't tried yet, so he decided to give it a try. He grabbed a few bags of different foods he didn't have in stock in case the raw kibble didn't work. He stopped to look at the treats knowing Maverick would eat those, but he couldn't eat only treats. Dan resolved to keep trying with different brands and types of food until he found something Maverick would eat.

Back at the shop he put some of the raw kibble food in a dish and placed it in front of Maverick. The dog looked at the dish and back up at Dan without eating anything. Dan pushed the dish closer to him and received the same reaction. Dan sat down next to

Maverick and sighed. He picked up some of the food in his hand and tried offering it to Maverick. Surprisingly, the dog ate it. Dan kept offering more until he wouldn't eat any more. Maverick drank some water before lying down, and Dan closed the door and headed to the lobby.

"Yes!" he screamed.

The girl behind the counter jumped instantly by the surprise outburst.

"Oh, sorry. I finally got Maverick to eat," Dan replied.

"Great! What did the trick?"

"Raw kibble I picked up this morning. I was running out of options, so I'm glad something worked," he explained.

He continued to hand feed him and slowly started adding in the crushed antibiotics. He was late starting them but they had to be taken with food per the vet's instructions, and eating hadn't gone so well up until then. Surely a few days wouldn't hurt, and Maverick was finally eating a few times a day.

FOUR

Dan continued the hand feeding for another few days and tried to implement a dish into the routine. It received the same indifference as before, but every day Dan kept putting a small amount of food in it and less in his hand. He started holding his hand over the dish, then lower, until it was almost in the dish. After a few days of this routine, Maverick finally started eating out of the dish. Feeding was getting easier, but it wasn't foolproof.

Dan started using the dish exclusively by the end of the first week, but he had to stay standing still and quiet or the dog would stop eating. He continued adding the antibiotics to the food and applying the ointment every day. Maverick's wounds didn't look much better, but Dan knew it would take some time before he saw an improvement. Maverick still acted wary in public, although Dan didn't take him many places other than the shop and home. Dan didn't want anyone to think he treated his dogs like that, and he was ashamed for Maverick to be in such a condition. He also felt the dog should be able to keep what little dignity he had left and build his confidence back up.

Since the previous owners claimed the dog didn't behave properly around children, Dan was nervous about introducing Maverick to his young daughter.

Being at home every night with the family, Maverick was slowly becoming less shy. He started spending time with Dan's daughter and was very affectionate. He seemed to enjoy the attention he was getting, and the house was soon filled with giggles and smiles. His tail wagged as he covered the little girl in kisses, and he started following her around the house wherever she would go. She was amused by this and would giggle every time she turned around to find Maverick just a step behind.

Maverick could be found sleeping in the bed at night and turned out to be quite a fan of snuggling. Most of Dan's Weimaraners were like this, and he was pleased to see Maverick coming out of his shell.

The dog started getting involved more at the shop. He would socialize with other dogs, play outside around the many slides and toys, and run the yard in the back with Dan's other dogs. There were so many dogs running in the back at times it looked more like herding than exercise and play. Maverick would make the rounds inside the shop visiting the various boarders and residents. He was especially fascinated and excitedly inquisitive when it came to the smaller dogs. He would visit them while they were at the shop. Dan would occasionally see Maverick on one of the sofas, but his favorite spot was still on the rug he picked out from the first week he arrived. He was becoming more social, more affectionate, and most importantly, more trusting.

Another month had passed and Maverick's wounds were healing. He was gaining weight, his skin infections were healing well, and his bones weren't protruding as much. He had finished his antibiotics two weeks before, and his follow-up visit with the vet came sooner than Dan imagined. They headed back on the same drive as a month before.

This time was different, though. Maverick walked in with his tail wagging, and the girls at the front desk were thrilled to see him again. They remembered when he had first come in, and they could not stop commenting on how great he looked. Dan sat down to wait for his appointment and recalled sitting there the first time with Maverick. He had felt so worried and had felt the stares from others in the lobby burn through his chest. Now he was receiving compliments, and Maverick was no longer frightened.

Dan relived the recent history in his mind until it was time to go into the examination room. When his name was called, he headed down the hall with Maverick. Upon reaching the room, the vet was already inside and waiting.

"Whoa, this isn't the same dog!" he exclaimed. The vet patted Maverick on the head and looked over his body.

"He's filling out good, Dan. Putting on some weight, muscles regaining some strength. I'd say in another month you might not even notice this dog was malnourished."

The vet examined his nose and chest to check the progress of the sores and infections.

"You must have been vigilant with the medicine. These areas look really good. His paws and tail are healing well too."

He listened to Maverick's heart with his stethoscope, felt his body in different areas, and checked his temperature.

"Any concerns, anything out of the ordinary with his recovery?" the vet asked Dan.

"Nope. He hasn't had any setbacks, he's eating regularly, and his initial shyness has really improved. He's at the shop during the day and home with me at night getting an extra meal. He gets along with everyone and every dog, and I haven't noticed any behavioral issues. He's definitely not the same dog I brought in here a month ago."

"Certainly not, that's for sure. Keep using the ointment and Vitamin E, but I don't see a need to start any more antibiotics right now. Keep doing what you're doing, and bring him back in another month." The vet patted Maverick on the head and showed Dan to the front desk to set the next appointment.

Dan continued the same regimen for the next few weeks, and he noticed Maverick was filling out better than he anticipated. The dog was happy and alert, and he was eating normally like the other dogs. He walked with dignity and almost commanded attention in his movements, and it seemed a sense of grace was about him. Dan remembered the papers that he had received a week after he brought Maverick home. He had forgotten about them until now, and he went in his office to find them.

Dan didn't know what he was looking at, but he scanned the papers to find out what they could tell him about Maverick. He noticed a breeder section, and there was a name and contact information. Most breeders have an agreement that their dogs are returned to them instead of being sold or given away, and Dan thought about making contact. He wondered if the breeder would demand the dog be returned. Dan had no intention of giving him up, but he knew if he was the breeder he would want to know Maverick's location and condition.

He reluctantly picked up the phone and started dialing. He took a few deep breaths as the phone rang, and after a few rings there was an answer.

"Hello?" a woman answered.

"Hi there, my name's Dan and I believe I have one of your dogs. A friend of mine found him in an ad for sale and contacted me. I run a Weimaraner rescue and agreed to meet with the dog. I bought him from the owner, but he was in real bad shape. I wanted to see who I could talk to about him."

"Well I'm Jan, and I'm the breeder," she replied. "What is the dog's name?"

Dan fumbled through the paperwork while explaining, "His name is Maverick, but I'm trying to find his AKC name on this…"

She cut him off before he could explain further. "Maverick? Oh my goodness, I've been trying to track him down for so long now. The original owner moved without a forwarding address and left me no idea of how to contact him or check in on the dog. Wait, where are you?"

"I'm in Virginia."

"Good grief, that dog traveled far. We're on the west coast in Canada! Well, I am so glad you called. How is he?" she asked.

"He wasn't great when I got him." Dan ran through the list of conditions and problems Maverick had, as well as explained how long it took to get him to eat and overcome his shyness. Dan could hear her gasps as he described the sores, overgrown nails, and protruding bones.

"That is not how Mav left us. He was happy, healthy, and was already earning ribbons in the show ring. What in the world did they do to him?"

"I'm not sure, but I thought you should know I have him now. He has recovered very well and finished the antibiotics, but I'm still applying ointment and vitamins to his skin to help heal the wounds. I was hoping you could tell me more about him. I'm not into the show scene, so I don't know what I'm supposed to do with him in that area. Do I train, get him a handler or someone to take him to shows, or what? His recovery has progressed better than I expected, and I'd like to give him a chance to do the shows if he enjoys them."

Dan never turned down a Weimaraner in need, but his experience was limited to his services and rescue efforts. Maverick seemed destined for more, but Dan didn't know what that entailed.

"Oh he loved the shows. He did great when he was a puppy," she explained, "and he took to the ring like a seasoned pro. His dad was a best of breed at the Westminster Kennel Club dog show, did you know? It's one of the oldest sporting events in the nation."

"Best of breed? I apologize, but I'm not familiar with what any of that means," Dan said.

She explained that best of breed was a title given to the dog best representing the specifications of a particular breed. Out of all the Weimaraners at the show, Maverick's dad was chosen as the best representation of the breed from all the dogs evaluated at the show. The title is highly sought after among breeders. It makes them more desirable for breeding stock as well.

"Oh okay, I've heard of that before." He checked his watch and continued, "I'm sorry to cut this short, but I need to get going. Can we exchange contact information and discuss this more in-depth another time?"

"Yes, please. I would love to hear more about him and figure out where he's been. I'm glad he's in good hands now."

They exchanged their contact information with an agreement to speak more over the weekend. Dan was pleased to be in contact with her and glad she didn't ask for the dog to be returned. The show information sounded serious and complicated, but he'd find out more about that later. For now it was time to get Maverick and head home.

Dinner time at home was much easier than before, and he fed Maverick before heading to his computer. He wasn't sure what he was looking for, so he just started searching for Virginia dog shows. Most of the results were reports on the winners of the shows or other news articles, so he tried to refine the search to include only upcoming dog shows. He was able to find a local show at the end of May. It coincided with a dock diving event he had that same weekend, but as he understood it he wouldn't actually go with the dog. That was the handler's job, though he wasn't entirely sure what that entailed either. He made a note of the date and location and would look into it tomorrow.

The next day at the office was busy but slowed in the afternoon. He remembered the show and started thinking about handlers. He guessed he had better find one to get started making some calls to see if anyone had a suggestion. He also did a few searches and contacted a few of them before reaching Darlene. She was familiar with handling Weimaraners and agreed to meet. She and Dan set a meeting for the next day, and it would prove to be another informative and surprising visit.

As soon as Darlene saw the dog, she knew she had seen him before. "I know this dog. A family brought him to me and asked me to show him not too long ago."

"Oh, so you've shown him before?"

"No," she continued, "this dog was in poor health, and the little kid they had with them was torturing this poor guy. The kid was rough with him, to the point of tormenting him. Maverick looked miserable, and I refused to handle him until his health and care improved."

Dan was surprised the family had tried to show him in that condition. "It sounds like the people I got him from. He was in real bad shape—sores, infections, grossly underweight, overgrown nails, you name it. It's taken me two months to get him looking like this."

"Well, I have to say he looks a million times better than he did. He filled out nicely and isn't hanging his head down constantly."

She squatted next to the dog to have a closer look, and as she looked him over she received a wet tongue to the face.

"Hi, big guy. I remember you." She checked his neck, shoulders, back, legs, and tail before standing up.

"He looks really good, Dan, and his demeanor is so different from before. It's a huge improvement. I'll show him for you. What show did you have in mind?"

"There's a local one coming up," he said as he fumbled for the papers he had printed.

"Ah, yes, at the end of May. We can get him in for that one. It's a few weeks away, so I'm sure he'll look even better by then. We'll have to get him ready for the show experience, though, so we have some work to do."

"See, that's what I don't understand. What is the show experience? What does he have to do?" Dan was puzzled and felt silly for asking.

"No," she laughed, "it's things like running or gaiting beside me and stacking—standing still, focused and confident while being evaluated. The dogs are usually seen by a judge with other dogs from the same breed, and it usually doesn't take that much time for the actual judging. Unless, of course, the judge can't decide between two dogs. Or someone calls the wicket on him, and that can cause problems."

"Wicket?"

"Yeah, it's a measuring device to make sure the dog meets or doesn't exceed the height standard for the breed. It looks like a piece from a metal walker. The legs are adjusted to the height the dog needs to be, and the judge slides it over the dog where the shoulders meet the neck to make sure the height meets the standard of the breed. If both legs touch the ground, the dog's too short and will be disqualified. If one leg doesn't reach, the dog is allowed back in.

"Sometimes the dog can be slouching or not feeling well and look shorter than normal. Other times handlers use it when they think another dog has a better chance of beating their dog. It's a risky move, and it can annoy the judge. Some judges even force the handler calling the wicket to have their own dog measured too. I haven't seen it often, but it has happened. We can measure Maverick and make sure he meets the breed standard before he goes to his first show."

Dan shook his head. "It sounds pretty serious. Am I out of my league here?"

"Just keep him happy, healthy, and practice with him. I'll show you what to do at home. When he's at the show, it's all down to me," she assured him.

"Thanks for seeing him and meeting with us. I'm a little nervous but excited to try something new, so let's give it a go."

They made arrangements for the next meeting where training would begin, and Dan couldn't help thinking about what she said as he drove back to the shop. The shows seemed to have the potential to become fierce with competition, and he wondered if it would have a negative effect on Maverick.

"Let's try one and see how you like it. What do you think?" he asked as he walked Maverick back into the shop. The dog looked up at him and wagged his tail, and Dan took that as a sign of approval.

They walked in and instantly got bombarded with questions.

"Well, how did he do?"

"Is he going to do the show?"

"What'd she say?"

Dan smiled, held his hands up and said, "He's going in."

The next meeting with Darlene came quickly, and Maverick's training soon began. Darlene instructed Dan on how to train him at home, and he wasted no time getting started. Most of it involved walking on a lead, running alongside Dan, and being able to stack when needed. There was also the possibility of him being evaluated, so they practiced that as well. When they weren't practicing, Maverick would be playing outside or sleeping on his favorite rug in the lobby.

SIX

Everything was going according to plan. Maverick's skin looked healed, he gained more weight, and he was doing great with the practices. Overall he seemed like a happy, healthy dog, and Dan was proud of how well he endured considering his history.

The other Weimaraner rescues had been practicing on the dock for their upcoming show. Dan loved seeing them dive and swim. They looked so happy and always raced back to the dock to do it again. The dock diving competitions were fun, and the dogs enjoyed being able to mingle with the people and dogs at the event. Dan was excited as usual, but he was nervous for Maverick. He worried constantly that Maverick would get freaked out, be intimidated, or shut down again. It was only one show and if that happened, it would be Maverick's last.

Memorial Day weekend arrived faster than Dan expected, and it was time to head out with the dogs on Friday. He dropped Maverick off to Darlene before going to the dock diving event.

"I think I am more nervous than he is," he told her as he handed over the lead.

"Ah, he'll be fine. He's done great so far, and I'm sure today will be no exception. Go have fun, and we'll see you after the show."

As Dan went to tell Maverick goodbye, the dog turned around and jumped up to give him a hug. He placed his front paws on Dan's shoulders, and their heads touched for a moment before he hopped down and looked up at him as if to say, "Don't worry. I got this." Darlene led him away and Dan just stood there feeling overwhelmed for a minute before returning to his truck to make the nine-hour drive to the dogs at the other event.

Dan watched the dogs dive off the dock one after another, but he couldn't help thinking of Maverick. He wondered how the show was going and how he was doing. He checked his watch a few times too many, and time seemed to crawl. He convinced himself that if he didn't look at the time, it would fly by faster. He would check again only to find five minutes had passed. The waiting was torture, and he was glad when it was time to head back.

He actually left the dock diving event early to head back and sneak into the show on the last day. He saw Darlene after the show and she was smiling, so Dan took that as a good sign.

"How'd he do? Everything go okay?"

"Not bad for his first time out with me," she replied.

"Hey, that's something! Was he nervous or scared?"

"Nah, he really did great. Stop worrying, Dan. He's fine, and I think he actually enjoyed it. The other dogs were firm and standing at attention, and it was funny to look over every now and then and see his tail start wagging."

Dan breathed a sigh of relief. He rubbed and patted Maverick and asked him if he had fun.

Maverick's tail was moving wildly, and he was excited to run back to the truck to see the other dogs again. She waited until he was out of earshot to continue like adults do with children when talking about them.

She continued, "I will tell you, there were only two Weimaraners that showed including him, so second place was pretty much a guarantee for him unless the judge liked him more than the other dog."

"He does seem happy though, and it's a good experience for him at least. Same time tomorrow?" Dan asked.

"Yep, every day. Monday is the last day, and the schedule should be the same until the end.

"See you tomorrow then." Dan thanked her and headed back to the shop.

The next three days passed quickly, and Maverick placed second every single day. Dan made it back early for the last day and was able to see Maverick being handled in the main ring. He watched the judge walk back and forth in front of the dogs, studying them carefully before pointing them to another position. He pointed to Maverick second, so that must have meant he took second place again. Dan still had a lot to learn, and he was sure he'd pick it all up in time.

After the show Darlene confirmed he had won second place again.

"It's a good start for him to be out here. There were not as many dogs here as some competitions, but the fact that he was seen and enjoyed it is a good sign," she said.

"There's another show next month. It's a few hours away in Charlottesville, and I'm going to be there handling another dog. What do you think about putting

Maverick in it? It's a bigger show with more competition, but I think he can handle it."

Dan thought about it for a minute.

"Well, if there are more Weimaraners in that show, we'll be able to see how he places out of all of them?"

"There should definitely be more Weimaraners at that show. I'd suggest giving it a shot."

Dan agreed. "As long as he is still happy and having fun like he did this weekend, one more show won't hurt. I can make arrangements to drive there with him and stay for the show. He can't go alone or be left in a crate for any length of time because of his previous situation."

Dan thought about the travel aspect for a minute and asked, "Do most of the shows require travel?"

"If you want him in a show, you have to go where the show is—and that requires travel," she advised.

"Because of his history, I'm not sure a full show schedule is possible. I wanted to be able to offer this to him for fun, but I won't continue showing him if it means he will suffer in any way. I'm just not sure about the impact it might have on him."

"You said you can drive the three hours, right? So come to this next show with him and give him a shot. See where he places with a bigger group."

"Okay."

"Great," she said. "Call me this week for the details and keep practicing with him. He lowered his rear end a few times when the judge touched him, so focus on getting people he's not familiar with to do the same."

Dan said he would, thanked her, and headed back to the truck.

More training was done in the weeks that followed. Maverick saw new people and animals every day as clients came in for boarding, so Dan had different people practice examining him so the dog would get used to being touched. He would practice while Maverick was standing on the floor or on a small platform, and at first he did lower his rear and try to sit. The more they practiced, the easier it was for Maverick to remain standing.

SEVEN

The next show was approaching, and Maverick was still looking better every week. It was hard to tell this dog had been through anything short of a lavished lifestyle. While watching him stand as a client ran his hands over his back and raised the tail, Dan noticed that the dog didn't move this time. Not an inch.

"Good boy!" he yelled out as he walked over to him. Maverick's tail was moving wildly as he ran over and jumped up to give Dan one of his signature hugs.

Dan had talked to Jan after the last show, and she told him about the shows he did as a puppy. He performed extremely well, was never shy, and would get really excited before and after a show. She was excited to hear that Maverick was enjoying it again, and that he was finally moving past the neglect and abuse he had suffered just four months earlier. She wished Dan luck and made him promise to call her after the next show.

The day had arrived for the show. Dan was excited because he would be able to stay and watch this time. He packed up the truck and started the three-hour trip to Charlottesville. Maverick was happy to lie around and enjoy the ride, and the hours passed quickly. Before he realized it, he was at the highway exit and the show grounds soon after.

They found Darlene, and Dan asked where he should wait.

"Anywhere along the ringside area is fine. I'm showing another dog, but I'll have someone with Maverick at all times."

"No crates."

"Nope, no crates," she confirmed.

Dan was relieved but knew she would take good care of him. It was probably silly of him to ask, but he was overly cautious when it came to Maverick.

It was pretty hot that day, but it was June after all. He found a place to watch among other fans, and he listened to their chatter while waiting to see Maverick and Darlene somewhere in the show.

It was an outdoor show and there were multiple rings set up, so Dan wasn't even sure where to look. He watched the dogs and their handlers make the rounds and stand at attention for the judges. His friend Sarah joined him as he was waiting. She was there showing one of her dogs and was pretty excited about seeing Maverick there.

An hour had passed and still no sign of Maverick. It wasn't long before they called for the Weimaraners, and soon there were nine of them being lined up just outside the judging ring. Maverick stood statuesque in the ring and looked like he belonged in there with the other dogs.

Dan could see Maverick looking in his direction and pulling on the lead. His tail was wagging and front paws moving around as if to get a better view.

"Excuse me—Dan?" he heard a few minutes later, accompanied by a tap on the shoulder.

"Yes?"

"We're going to need you to leave the ringside area," she said. "Maverick can't focus because he can sense you."

"I have to leave?" Dan asked with a painful look on his face.

"Unfortunately, yes. I know you're new at this and so is Maverick, but until he is able to focus we do need you to keep your distance. This is common and happens often with our new clients."

"Okay."

Dan felt deflated. This was Maverick's second show and a bigger one, and he wouldn't get to watch. He walked around the crowd then behind it. He could barely see anything, but he wanted Maverick to do well.

Dan felt sad, but at the same time he was happy that Maverick was looking for him. He felt like he did at the last dock diving competition while Maverick was in his first show. Checking his watch every five minutes, pacing, and making a few phone calls was all he could do to remain calm.

He started walking around the show rings to watch the other breeds and pass the time. As he rounded the edge of one ring, he was startled when something flew in front of his foot. He scrunched his eyebrows in confusion as he looked down to find what appeared to be a piece of a hot dog. He stood back up and looked to the right to find dogs circling the ring for judging.

There was a line of handlers standing with their dogs to the right while the remaining dogs were circling back around. He saw something else fly across the ring, and he was stunned.

A handler in the line was throwing pieces of hot dogs to the dogs still circling the ring. One of the dogs pulled away from his handler in an effort to retrieve the treat, and the handler tried to get his focus back as they approached the rear of the line. Another handler picked up a piece of the hot dog and threw it at yet another handler.

Dan was speechless at the food fight that was occurring before his eyes. He wondered if this was considered normal behavior, and he really hoped he would never have to contend with that kind of fiasco.

After what seemed like an eternity, he saw Darlene and Maverick walking away from the judging ring. He leaped into position to meet them.

"Hey boy!" he called out to Maverick as he walked up. Maverick's tail set off wagging again when she interrupted.

"Whoa, don't get him too excited."

"Why not? He's done, right?"

"Nope. We have to go back in, but it's a good thing. He won the class, winner's dog, best of winners, and the best of breed. Now he heads to the sporting group."

"Best of class and breed, and does he get points for those?"

"Yes, he placed ahead of the others in the show and he gets points toward champion."

Dan was excited about the breed but was unsure what the other names meant.

Darlene walked up to Dan, and there was another woman with her.

"Dan, this is Brittany. She's going to take Maverick for the sporting group portion. My other dog placed, so I need to be there for the extra judging rounds."

"Okay." Dan introduced himself to Brittany and quickly explained Maverick's history. He told her about the last show and how he had hunkered down his rear end.

"We practiced it before the show and he's gotten better at it."

"I'm sure he'll be fine," she said. "We'll be back after the judging is finished."

Dan watched her walk away and returned to his previous position.

He headed back to where Sarah was watching.

"So, how did he do?" she asked.

"He won class and breed, and two other things I'm not sure of. I know class is his age or group and breed is out of the other Weimaraners, but what are winner's dog and best of winners?"

Sarah laughed.

"He won best in his class, right? So then he competes against the Weimaraners that won their classes. It's the winners against each other. He won that, and that's called winner's dog. That's out of the male Weimaraners. The females are judged separately in their classes the same way, and one of them is also chosen as winner's dog. Then the male and female that won the winner's dog compete against each other. The winner of that is called best of winners. Maverick was chosen as the best breed example out of every other male and the best female Weimaraner here, and he should be heading to the group competition next."

"Yes, sporting group, she said."

"Yep, that's the next round. If he wins there, he'll continue on. If not, you're done for the day."

"Oh, okay. Sorry, but this is all new to me."

"No problem," she laughed. "It takes some getting used to, and the terminology can be confusing at first. Luckily you have me here to explain it all."

"You may have to explain this to me again, you know."

"Hey, what are friends for?" she replied. He laughed and agreed.

EIGHT

Sarah and Dan turned their attention to the dogs in the various judging rings. Dan could barely see Maverick but was excited about him being judged best in something. Dan already knew he was one incredible dog, and he was glad about the recognition and attention Maverick was getting.

The waiting and watching was difficult for Dan. He didn't always have a good view because he had to hide under or behind vendor tents so the dog wouldn't notice him. Dan was nervous watching Maverick with the other breeds in the sporting group for the first time. He watched the judge slowly examine each dog and look over them again in the lineup, and Dan recognized him as the same judge who had chosen Maverick for best of breed.

Maverick looked like he belonged in the group. His stance was just as poised as the other dogs, and Dan was getting butterflies just thinking about Maverick being selected from such an amazing group of dogs.

A little while later he saw Brittany walking back with Maverick, and he headed over to meet them again. Maverick was still wagging his tail and excited, and Dan couldn't wait to hear what else had happened.

"He didn't place in the sporting group," Brittany explained, "but they took his best of breed picture with Darlene. They couldn't get him to stand and didn't want to stress him out, so they let him sit."

"He looks happy as can be. No stress there, eh Mav?" he asked as he rubbed his ears. Dan turned back to Brittany and asked about future handling possibilities since Darlene had prior commitments coming up for a few months.

Brittany replied, "I'm an assistant to Rusty, and if you plan on showing him again then he will take over, but sure, we'd be glad to help. He's such a nice dog and I'd love to see him with us again."

"I hadn't really thought about it, to tell you the truth. I figured if he didn't place here or have a good time, this would be his last show. Now that he has these ribbons and seems happy, maybe I should consider letting him do it again."

"I think you'd be silly not to enter him again. He received points today for those wins, and you might be able to get enough for champion."

Dan was puzzled. "What do you mean by points?"

Sarah had walked up just a moment before and interrupted.

"Sorry, Brittany, he's not familiar with all of the aspects of dog shows." She turned to Dan, "When Maverick won those classes he was also awarded points. Those points are added together with wins from major competitions and count toward him being named a champion of his breed. So if you decided to continue and he won more classes, he might get more points and become a champion. Beyond that it's grand champion."

Dan thought about this for a minute. "He's having fun, so that's not a factor. But what about travel? I have to be able to drive him and stay with him or he doesn't go."

"The next show is in Ohio and it's a major, so if you can make it he might get more points," Brittany explained. "I'll have Rusty get in contact with you about the details."

"Sure, it's worth considering. Thanks for handling him today, he looks like he had fun and really likes you."

Just before they were about to say goodbye, Brittany told him something the judge had said while he was in the ring: "Your dog caught my eye as soon as he walked into my ring."

Dan asked, "He said that? That's good, right?"

"That was one of the judges. That's a great compliment."

"Short and sweet, but hey, I'll take it!" Dan thanked Brittany again for handling him in the show.

"Oh it was my pleasure."

Dan was excited about the show and called Jan to tell her the good news. She was happy it was a good experience and asked if Dan had gotten Maverick's clearances done yet.

"Clearances?" Dan asked. "What are those?"

"Clearances are medical tests that evaluate the dog for health issues, defects, or anything that might cause a problem in health and breeding. They check the hips, elbows, heart, thyroid, eyes, and more to make sure he won't pass down a genetic disorder or have a health issue. Each breed has health issues they are prone to getting, and this helps keep the breed standard intact. The goal is to identify and eliminate genetic disorders by having these thorough screenings done and uphold ethical standards. It's also a good idea to have them done to see where he's at health-wise to uncover any unknown issues. If you haven't done them yet, it's probably a good idea to get them," she explained.

"No, he hasn't had anything like that. It sounds like it could be helpful, so I'll definitely look into it. There was a vet at the show and I had him check Maverick's heart, and he said he couldn't find any issues. He did tell me to follow up with my vet to have more tests done, so I'll schedule those soon."

"Sounds great. Keep me updated."

The conversation with Jan had him thinking about Maverick's health. The dog was emaciated for some time, and Dan wondered if that had an effect on any part of his body. Sure, the vet had given him a clean bill of health for parasites and worms, but what about internal organs? What if there was permanent damage done? One alarming condition common for Weimaraners was malabsorption syndrome. This condition can be difficult to manage. The dog's body doesn't digest the food properly and the nutrients are not absorbed. It can also be a hereditary condition and is usually treated with specialized food. What if Maverick had that too? Dan resolved himself to get the rest of the tests done just to be sure there wasn't anything to worry about.

Maverick was back in the vet's office to get the remainder of his tests done. He had to be under anesthesia for the tests and the X-rays. Dan was uneasy about Maverick being under anesthesia. He wondered if the dog had ever been under anesthesia, how he might react, and was worried about potential complications.

The tests and recovery took half the day, and as soon as Maverick was walking around Dan headed back home. He helped the dog out of the car and noticed how he walked slowly as he wobbled slightly toward the door. Dan went through his usual routine of setting out Maverick's food and checking the mail. He went to search on the computer about breeding and issues with Weimaraners, and he found some information about the tests and why they are important.

There were many regulatory organizations that issued the clearances he was told about, and he hoped Maverick's would all come back okay. He hadn't realized how much time had passed while he was in the office, and he went to check on Maverick. His food dish was sitting there still full. Dan assumed he wasn't hungry and called it a night.

NINE

The morning was oddly familiar. Dan woke to find Maverick's dish still untouched, and he desperately hoped that Maverick would eat at some point in the day. The sight of the full dish made his heart sink. Going back to the problems he had eating initially would be devastating to his progress. They headed in to the shop for the day's work and Dan left food for him in his office. He checked a few times throughout the day and the food remained untouched. This was the second day since the X-rays and Maverick still had not eaten anything. Dan tried shaking the dish and moving it closer to him, and the dog just looked at him.

"Not again. Come on boy, you have to eat."

Maverick just lowered his head and looked away. Dan felt helpless. He looked sadly at the dog and wondered why this was happening. He was scared at the idea of Maverick not eating again. How long would this last? How much weight will he lose? How much could he afford to lose? Dan knew he was once again in frightening territory and needed to get Maverick eating again as soon as possible.

These concerns swirled in Dan's head as he headed into the lobby to finish up any remaining items needing his attention so he could get Maverick home.

He grabbed a bag of treats on the way out, collected the dog, and drove home.

Once there he tried the dish with dog food again to see if Maverick would eat. It was the same reaction as before, so he removed the dish and retrieved the bag of treats. He left a few in front of Maverick, who promptly ignored them. Dan put a few treats in his hand and held it out for him, but Maverick still wouldn't eat. He just backed up and lay down looking in the other direction.

When Maverick looked away, Dan turned his gaze to the bag of dog treats. He studied the ingredients and pretended to ignore Maverick to see if he would seek attention. The dog didn't budge, but Dan realized the treats in his hand were not the same ones as the first time he got Maverick to eat. He decided to let him rest for the night; he would pick up the familiar treats tomorrow and try again.

On his way into work the next morning, Dan tried to figure out why Maverick had regressed. The only thing different in his routine was the anesthesia for the tests, and he hadn't been the same since. He called the vet when he arrived at the shop and confirmed that the procedure of being put under was a likely cause for his stress.

"He should start eating again soon. If he doesn't, bring him in," the vet advised.

"Thanks. I'm going to try one more thing and if that doesn't work, expect to see us this afternoon."

Dan found the brand of treats he had used the first time, and he went into his office to see if they would work. Initially Maverick was uninterested as usual, but Dan put a few treats in his hand and held it toward him anyway. He saw his nose start to twitch as the dog inhaled the new smell around him, and he turned toward Dan's hand to make a closer inspection. Maverick shyly took one of the treats and ate it, smacking his lips. He immediately looked up for more treats, and Dan happily obliged as the dog continued to eat the rest.

"It's like that again, eh?" Dan asked him. Maverick just looked up at him and back at his hand for any remaining treats.

"Okay, okay, but you can't eat treats all day."

Dan fed him a few more handfuls and mixed some into his food dish. He had to follow the same routine as in the beginning: hand feeding, mixing canned food, and slowly directing Maverick back toward his regular food. It was a slow process that took another two days, but at least he was back to eating again. Things felt like they were returning to normal, and later that week the vet called to check on him. He was glad to hear Maverick was eating again. He also told Dan he expected the tests for the clearances to come back with high ratings since Maverick's hips appeared tight and the dog appeared to be in excellent health now.

Rusty called a few days later with the details on the next show. It was in August and Dan was able to bring Maverick that weekend. He agreed to the show and made arrangements with Rusty for the day it started.

"Should I keep practicing with him? With the standing and touching, or is it unnecessary now?"

"I would keep doing it. It gets him used to it, and there's another month before the show. See you then."

Dan noticed a message waiting and checked his voice mail. The message was from Maverick's vet with the results of his clearances. Everything came back normal and his hips were ranked in the top 10 percent. The vet said it was good news but to call him if Dan had any questions. Dan was relieved that no other issues were present.

The last few months had been a whirlwind for Dan. From Maverick's rehabilitation to the dog show excursions, it was hard to believe it all happened in the manner of just four months. Once he had become comfortable with the aspects of handling again, Maverick seemed to embrace it. Dan wondered if he remembered being in shows when he was a puppy and was drawing from those experiences.

He also wondered how far Maverick would have gotten if he hadn't been mistreated so badly. He remembered how awful he had looked on the first day they met. The family wasn't concerned at all for the dog and looked at him as a burden. His next stop could have been a worse owner or a shelter, and the thought still disgusted Dan. He was an entirely different dog now; happy, healthy, and had an incredible personality. Another show was on the horizon, and Dan knew the time would pass by quickly.

The next few weeks were business as usual, until one morning Dan woke up to find bumps and hives all over Maverick's back. He had no idea what had caused the bumps, although several possibilities ran through his head. Bug bites, something venomous, or an allergic reaction were some ideas as Dan brainstormed. He was scared they would spread or intensify.

He examined the top and sides, and they were everywhere. He called Rusty to cancel the show and scheduled an appointment at the vet's office. Whatever the bumps were, they must have been itching. Maverick kept scratching, and Dan was worried he'd make it worse or create even more irritation. He tried to keep him from scratching until they left.

As soon as they sat down at the vet's office, Maverick started scratching again. Dan kept him from scratching until they were called in to an examination room.

"What seems to be the trouble today?" the vet asked while looking over Maverick.

"He has bumps all over and keeps scratching."

The vet checked Maverick's vital signs and examined the bumps. They were uniformly scattered across the back.

"Have you changed his food lately?" he asked.

Dan shook his head. "No, his food is the same."

"What about outdoor areas? Has he been anywhere new lately where he might have brushed up against something?"

Again Dan shook his head.

"Have you changed his shampoo or started using anything new?"

"No," Dan replied, "I haven't changed anything. I checked the other dogs, and Mav is the only one with bumps."

"Has he ever had this before?"

Dan couldn't remember ever seeing Maverick with bumps or any other kind of reaction. "Nope, nothing."

"It looks like it could be bug bites or an allergic reaction, but if you haven't changed anything I imagine it will clear up soon. Keep an eye on the other dogs while you're treating him."

He suggested using an antihistamine to treat the reaction.

"Try to keep him from scratching if you can, and if it doesn't clear up in a few days, bring him back in."

Dan agreed to check in with him if Maverick didn't improve. He stopped at a store on the way back to the shop. He only needed a generic over-the-counter antihistamine, and those were common enough to find quickly. He made his way back to the shop and gave Maverick his first pill. Crushing it up in his food hadn't always been well received, so he put it on the back of his tongue and held his mouth closed until he swallowed it. This continued for a few days.

Dan was so worried that he found himself unable to sleep through the night. He kept waking up and checking on Maverick, who would often be sleeping and probably wondered why he was being bothered. This continued for a week while he monitored the dog's condition.

TEN

Maverick seemed to be acting normal with no signs of any other affliction, and Dan was keeping an eye on him so he didn't scratch too much. The bumps were not going away, so Dan made another appointment to return to the vet's office.

The results were the same as before: there didn't seem to be anything else wrong with Maverick; continue the treatment and come back in another week if needed. Dan did as instructed and hoped it would clear soon. He double-checked the shampoo, food and other items, and nothing different was used. Without a change in the dog's routine, Dan thought it might have been a bug bite after all.

After a few days the bumps strangely disappeared, and it was just two days before the show. Dan was surprised and called Rusty to give him the news. They would be going to the show after all.

This time Dan was 50 yards away in the crowd. He had dropped off Maverick to Rusty and made sure to keep his distance. The show was another outdoor one in the heat, and it was his first time working with Rusty. Dan was anxious to see how this show would turn out, and he tried to find Maverick among the other dogs.

Once again the tap on the shoulder arrived.

"Dan, he can't focus. You're going to have to move out of sight and further away," he was told.

"Again?"

"I'm sorry, but it will get easier with more shows. Until then, you will have to stay out of sight," Rusty explained.

"All right," Dan said with a dejected sigh. He hung his head and walked away until he was sure he couldn't be seen. He also couldn't see much or tell what was going on, and he was sad to miss another chance to see Maverick in the show. This was the last day of the show, and he had already done so well. Maverick won reserve winner's dog on Saturday and winner's dog on Sunday.

It looked like the show was wrapping up, so Dan headed back to his truck. He saw Rusty walking toward him with a smile on his face.

"He won a five-point major today," he said excitedly.

Dan was happy but a little confused, and he asked what a five-point major meant.

Rusty explained that five points were the maximum number of points that could be awarded at any show, and this show was considered a major because of the number of dogs entered. The more dogs that are entered into a show raise the total points that can be awarded. This show had a large number of dogs; therefore, the points available were the maximum of five.

"Why aren't all shows like this?"

Rusty continued, "It depends on the region as well. The number of dogs within a region can vary, so not all shows have a guaranteed number of dogs or points. Getting in a five-point major and winning really helps toward his total points."

He suggested that Dan bring him to the next show in North Carolina. It would be another major and might even result in Maverick becoming a champion if all went well. Hesitant as always, Dan asked him to send the details and he would consider it. He thought back to the vet visits and couldn't believe they almost missed the show. Weimaraners have very thin coats, and the bumps were very noticeable. He hoped they would not reappear and kept a close eye on everywhere Maverick went and everything he touched as much as possible.

The next show was in another week, and Dan figured he could make the trip. He had been practicing with Maverick for a few days, and it became so routine it probably bored the poor dog. Luckily, most of Maverick's days were filled with play and sleep, and he always received a great deal of attention from everyone. Regular clients would bring in their pets and ask how he was doing in the shows. Another client hadn't been there in a few months and was shocked to see Maverick in the lobby earlier that week. She even asked if it was the same dog and couldn't believe what a difference was made in just four months. Maverick loved the attention and affection. Dan thought about how serious he looked in pictures from the show, yet at the shop he was just like the other dogs: playful, sweet, and he always had a hug ready.

It was another hot August day, and Dan was on his way to the show. Maverick didn't seem to mind the drives much and was happy to lie around on the beds in the back or sneak up front from time to time. The drive wasn't bad, but it was longer than their previous trips. The directions estimated four and a half hours for the drive, and time went by quickly as usual.

They got settled in and drove over to the venue to meet Rusty. As Dan entered the show, it seemed chaos was in full swing. Tables and crates were lined in several long rows. The sound of hair dryers overwhelmed the many voices talking and the occasional barks from the dogs. Dogs large and small were on tables being primped and fluffed in preparation for their appearances. Dan's eyes widened as he braved past the bustling area to find Rusty.

The buzz from the staging area lowered to a faint echo as Dan made his way further into the event. He turned a corner and found Rusty – who grabbed the lead from Dan and was about to speak when Dan interrupted.

"I know, I know, get lost so he can't see me."

Rusty laughed and agreed, and said he would see him soon. Dan shuffled off to find a hiding place again. He found a place to stand but it didn't offer the best view. A flurry of handlers with dogs came rushing past him. Some of them excused themselves, while others just glared at him and brushed him out of the way. Dan looked around and was pretty sure he wasn't blocking a path. He had no idea why some of the handlers had rudely pushed him aside. He was already nervous about the show, and these altercations didn't help his anxiety.

This was an important show; it was a major and if Maverick placed well, the chance to become a champion loomed. Dan was still a bit frenzied by it all. He still looked back at Maverick's first day and found it hard to believe where he ended up. He enjoyed going to the shows and seeing the excitement in Maverick, but it always wrenched his stomach when he had to leave. He knew it was better for Maverick, but that didn't make it any easier.

Winner's dog and best of winners was the verdict on the first day. Those wins afforded more points to Maverick, and they were certainly worth celebrating. Another day of judging remained, so Rusty cautioned Dan not to get his hopes up.

"He still has to get through tomorrow and if all goes well, you might have a champion on your hands."

Dan let that sink in for a moment. Maverick is a champion. He still couldn't believe the same dog that cowered from strangers and endured such physical pain could be happy and healthy, much less a champion. He let out a huge sigh and thanked Rusty for a great first day. Maverick was excited as usual with his tail wagging furiously, and then headed back to get some sleep before the next day.

ELEVEN

Maverick had wins but not a title. He was placed in the open class because of this, but Dan didn't know how that factored into his odds for placement. As long as Maverick was happy, he was happy, but he did get excited every time another win was announced.

Sunday was no exception. Dan was hiding in the wings as usual, and Rusty returned with great news.

"Congratulations, Dan, you have a champion!"

Dan's mouthed dropped as he looked down at Maverick. "What?!"

"You heard me," Rusty said. "He took winner's dog and best of winners again today, and he acquired enough points to be classified as a champion."

"Way to go, Mav!" Dan said in celebration. He returned his attention to Rusty.

"I can't believe it. I mean, I always thought of him as a winner because he's such an amazing dog, but that's really incredible to add 'champion' next to his name. Yeah," he said, looking down at Maverick. "I'd say 'champion' suits him just fine."

Rusty knew Dan wasn't as familiar with the show titles, so he tried to explain the importance of what had just taken place.

"It's not just a fancy title. As a champion, Maverick won't have to go back to open class judging.

Champion means he goes straight to best of breed. That is, if you take him to any more shows."

"I've always said that as long as he is having fun, I'll take him to as many shows as possible. As long as he's with me for the travel and never crated, I can't deny this guy what he loves to do."

"I'm glad you said that," Rusty laughed, "because there is another show in September."

Dan looked up at him with a straight face. "Another show? Is there one a month or something? You guys are dragging me all over the place. Not that I mind, but this show business seems pretty continuous—and serious."

"For most people, it's a career or a way of life. Breeders with dogs that win titles are more sought after by people looking for a new puppy; some people do it for fun, others for status. It just depends on the individual. In your case, I'd say it's the fun factor all the way."

"I'd have to agree with that. If Maverick didn't enjoy it, we would have stopped months ago. He always seems to get excited before a trip, and he can't stop wagging his tail once he gets here. He's excited to see you too, so that's another bonus. But champion. Wow. That's awesome."

"Today paves the way for an easier ride for him in some classes, and fierce competition in others. The next one is in Raleigh, and we're talking major points. Beyond champion there's grand champion."

"What does grand champion consist of?"

"Something the kennel club folks came up with to keep the champions active and boost participation. It was just implemented in May and has another point schedule. If Maverick gets selected as best of breed, best of opposite or select dog, he will earn points toward the new title. Points are at the judge's discretion, of course, and he has to defeat at least one other champion at three shows. I'm sure he can do it, though, and Raleigh would be a good starting point. It's a bigger show and some people take it really seriously, but I wouldn't suggest it if I didn't know this guy would walk away with some points toward grand champion title. It's in the first week of September, so it's not far off. You want some time to think about it as usual?" Rusty joked, "Or can I count on making the drive to meet you?"

"He's happy. I'm happy. Let's do it."

They made plans to speak in a week to confirm the trip, and Dan made his way home with Maverick. A store caught his eye while he was driving, and he pulled over with a devious grin on his face. He parked and walked in to the store. After a few minutes, he emerged from the ice cream shop with a huge scoop of vanilla ice cream. He walked over to the side of the truck Maverick was on and opened the door. Dan held out the ice cream for Maverick to lick, but just as soon as the dog sniffed it he took a huge bite and the whole scoop was in his mouth. Dan laughed as Maverick sat there chewing the massive mound of ice cream with white drool running down his lips. He heard laughter and turned around, and other patrons were watching and pointing at Maverick. Dan just shrugged in response and laughed. He went back in to get more napkins and cleaned up before heading home again.

"Smooth sailing from here, eh Mav?" he called to the back of the truck. It would appear so, but the next show would prove to be a challenging experience.

Raleigh was a few hours away give or take the number of stops they made. Dan made the drive with Maverick leisurely hanging out in the back as usual. Dan was a little nervous this time around. Rusty had said this would be a bigger show with more competition, and Dan hoped it wouldn't be a bad experience for Maverick. He had done so well the past few months except for the eating issue that resurfaced. Dan hoped all of that was behind them for good as they pulled onto the show grounds.

TWELVE

September was still a warm month for the area, and it was a sunny day to start the Labor Day weekend. Dan parked the truck and headed inside with Maverick to find Rusty. The place was pretty big, and there were multiple rings roped off for simultaneous judging to take place. The crating and grooming areas were very tight quarters, and he felt bad for some of the dogs that needed more grooming. Luckily Maverick had short hair and didn't require much pampering, and Dan was glad they could avoid such a dilemma. He noticed Rusty across the room and navigated around the dogs and groomers to meet him.

"This is a big place."

"I told you it would be bigger," Rusty explained as he reached over to grab Maverick's lead. "How was the drive?"

"Easy and uneventful. Definitely shorter than Canfield." Dan looked around for the ringside area before Rusty could speak.

"I know the drill, go away."

Rusty laughed and said, "See you soon."

Dan took his place at what he thought would be a safe distance and watched the various rounds of the show. The time for the Weimaraner judging soon approached, and Dan felt a knot in his stomach. He was nervous for Maverick, always worrying if the dog was okay. His eyes followed the judge as he examined the dogs, and his heart felt like it was going to exit his chest whenever the judge was near Maverick. This show was just as unsettling and nerve-racking for Dan, while Maverick didn't seem to be affected at all.

The first day seemed to go by fast, and it wasn't long before he was meeting Rusty to collect Maverick.

"That was quick. How'd he do?"

Rusty smiled. "Select winner, not bad for day one. These points will count toward his grand champion title, so any win is good. He also placed second out of all the Weims, so that's impressive."

"Hey, that's great," Dan said as he rubbed Maverick's ears. "Points on the first day are always a good sign."

"Sure is. See you tomorrow, same time."

Dan headed back to the hotel with Maverick to get some rest. He made a few calls back home to share Maverick's first day and his new points. So far the trip was going well, and he hoped to get a few more points in before they had to leave. He searched on the internet for upcoming shows, and it looked like the next one wasn't until November in Virginia Beach. This meant no driving long distances and a month-long break for Maverick. Dan thought the break would be good for them both, unless Rusty knew of another show that didn't appear on the search results. He reminded himself to ask tomorrow and called it a night.

The next morning they headed back to the show and met with Rusty again. Dan worked his way to the ringside area and tried to find the same location he had stood in yesterday. Since there were no issues with Maverick seeing him, the same spot should be safe for this day as well. He watched the dogs in the various judging rings make their rounds. He knew from previous shows to watch for the judge to point at the dogs. This would mean that he was narrowing the top dogs to pick a winner or determining their placement. Sometimes a judge would ask the handlers to circle the ring again with the dogs. Dan guessed this was to see how well their movements were if the judge couldn't decide on appearance alone. It had all seemed so complicated in the beginning, but watching it now, he found it was easy to understand. That was until he noticed the Weimaraners being shown in another judging ring.

He noticed Rusty standing with Maverick, but his attention was on another handler. A woman walked up to someone inside the judging ring, but it was not the judge. He watched the man listening to the woman and seemed to ask if she was sure about something. The woman nodded her head, and the man started walking toward the judge. As the man talked privately with the judge, Dan noticed the judge move his head backward and reply. The man nodded in agreement and walked away in a hurry. The judge stood there and pointed to the dogs. Dan wasn't sure what was going on, but the dogs and the handlers were not moving.

People in the adjacent rings were starting to look over to the Weimaraner ring to see why there was no movement. All dog shows run on a schedule, so any delay pushes back every other dog and handler for the rest of the day. It has a cascading effect and pushes back the entire show. In what seemed like half an hour, the steward returned to the judge with what looked like pipes in his hand. The judge took them and started putting them together, although he was having trouble.

The man tried to assist him, and Dan noticed people were focused on what the judge was doing. He saw the item was almost finished being assembled and recognized it as the wicket.

Dan could not believe someone would call the wicket at a class full of champions, but he figured there must be a dog that looks too short or tall to be in the show. He had a sinking feeling that it might be Maverick, so he walked closer to the ring to get a better view of what was going on. People standing near him were commenting about the wicket and seemed to be in disbelief too. Dan heard several people saying that calling the wicket was certainly not the norm. Most judges can usually tell if a dog is within requirements, but they rarely call the wicket themselves because it is such a huge delay to everyone.

Dan looked back at the judge and noticed him pointing toward the handlers and motioning for one to come forward. He could not believe his eyes when he saw the dog that the judge was calling up was Maverick.

"Hey, that's Mav!" he exclaimed as he walked even closer to the ring. He wondered why the wicket was being used on Maverick.

He overheard a lady standing near him talking to another spectator.

"See that woman with the dog next to him? That's the one that went to talk to the man who went to get the wicket. She must have called for that dog to be measured. Either he looks out of requirements to her or she's scared he will beat her dog," she replied. "Either way, that's one risky move. Sometimes judges will make the handler have their dog measured too, just for the inconvenience, or they won't place their dog as a winner in any category."

"But what happens if he decides the dog doesn't measure correctly?" he heard the other person ask.

The woman replied, "If he decides the dog is out of the height range, you're talking disqualification and loss of points. I definitely wouldn't want to be his owner right now—or his handler."

Down in the ring Rusty had a look of disbelief on his face when he realized the judge was pointing to him. The other handlers were complaining loudly to the judge that the measuring was unnecessary, especially considering the dog was already a champion. The judge insisted he had to see it through and motioned again for Rusty to bring Maverick to him. Rusty eyed the woman next to him as he indicated for Maverick to walk with him.

THIRTEEN

The show seemed to be at a standstill. Everything was quiet. Everyone was quiet. The adjacent rings showed no movement. Everyone was watching the events unfold in the Weimaraner ring, and Dan still couldn't believe this was happening. Every show, every title, every point Maverick had earned—was it all at stake? They had worked so hard to get here, and he felt a knot in his stomach as he watched Rusty walk Maverick to the judge.

The judge motioned for Rusty to stack the dog, and once Maverick was in position the judge placed the wicket over him. Maverick was instantly spooked and backed away before running off. Rusty had to run after him to bring him back, and he was shying away while warily keeping an eye on the wicket. He acted strange, as if he could feel the tension around him and sense something unsettling about his surroundings. Rusty was worried he couldn't keep him there for measuring and that Maverick would be disqualified. Dogs that are not cooperative enough to be measured when attempted a few times are usually dismissed so that judging can continue. The handlers were still complaining from the line about the delay being caused, and luckily Maverick stayed in place the second time the judge used the wicket.

Dan was too far away to see what was going on. Spectators were stretching their necks in different directions trying to see the dog as the judge moved the wicket in different spots along the dog's back.

The judge stood up and started disassembling the wicket. He moved his hand to indicate to the ring steward to come forward and retrieve the wicket. He handed him the pieces, and the man walked away to return it. The judge straightened out his jacket and turned toward Rusty. He pointed at Maverick and then to the line of other Weimaraners to order Rusty back to his original position. Rusty breathed a sigh of relief and turned to get back in line. Upon seeing Maverick return to the lineup, the crowd erupted into applause.

Dan couldn't hear anything except the applause around him. He was relieved, and certainly never expected a dog show to be so stressful. He was glad Maverick was still in the show and judging would continue. Once he came down from the adrenaline high, he realized how close Maverick had come to losing everything he had worked toward. Dan breathed a sigh of relief and turned his attention back to the ring. Maverick was selected to stand out from the line of dogs, but Dan didn't know what this meant.

Rusty met Dan halfway from the spectator area shortly thereafter.

"I couldn't believe it," Dan told him.

Rusty looked relieved. "No kidding. I can't remember the last time I've seen the wicket called at a show, and I certainly didn't expect it to be called on Maverick at this point."

"Did you hear the applause?" Dan asked. "That was nuts."

"Yeah," Rusty continued, "that was stressful but I'm glad it's over. He took best of opposite."

Dan looked puzzled. "What does that one mean again?"

"The Weimaraner that won best of breed was a female, and Maverick was the best male to stand next to her. It also gets him some more points toward grand champion."

"That's good news then?"

"Yes, it's good news, and given the events of today it's nice to walk away with something for the headache. There's still a few more groups to go, but it's a win in my book."

Rusty headed back toward the ring with Maverick to finish out the day's events. A few hours later he met with Dan again and handed over Maverick's lead.

"Same time tomorrow?"

Rusty confirmed, "Yes same time, and hopefully tomorrow won't be as eventful as today."

The third day continued without incident, and Maverick was named select winner out of the other Weimaraners. He did not continue on to further judging, and Dan made arrangements to head home. He thanked Rusty for the weekend and hoped he would never see a repeat of the events from the show. Rusty confirmed the next show would be the November one Dan had read about, so they agreed to make contact near the end of October.

Dan was pleased to have a break from the show routine, and the next month consisted of playing and having fun with Maverick. Dan refined the dog's muscle mass with some extra exercise but made sure he didn't get too bulky. A few people thought Maverick looked better with five extra pounds, and some others thought the lesser weight was more attractive. Dan remembered how skinny Maverick was when he first got him, and he was still so surprised to be at a point where his weight was healthy enough to be adjusted. He had been so scared each time Maverick refused to eat that they would be back at the beginning trying to put weight on him.

Work continued at the shop and with the rescue, but time flew by fast. Before Dan knew it, Rusty was calling about the November show.

This show was a local one in Virginia Beach, and Dan was happy about not having to drive far. It was indoor and featured breed judging, obedience courses and junior handler competitions. This was a large show with prizes and ribbons, and a few specialty breeds would compete over the weekend. Rusty wouldn't be able to get there until Friday, so Dan made plans to attend on Thursday and handle Maverick himself.

FOURTEEN

The convention center was a big place, and after parking Dan went inside with Maverick. The sound of barking echoed throughout the tall corridors as he made his way into the interior of the building. He stopped at one ring where an obedience course was set up and handlers were taking their dogs through one at a time. It was a small course with a short wicker perimeter, and place cards on the ground indicated where each dog had to stop and obey a command. After watching for a few minutes, he headed further in to find the ring for breed judging.

Dan had seen Rusty and other handlers guide their dogs in the ring, so he had an idea of what to do when the time came. Soon he was walking Maverick up to the ring on the lead and getting into position. One by one the handlers walked their dogs around for the judge to view and returned to their place in line with the other handlers. The other Weimaraners were good-looking dogs, but Dan decided when looking at Maverick that he was the best one there. He wondered if he thought that because he was biased or if Maverick really did have an edge over the competition. The judged decided for him, and Maverick was directed to take a place alongside two other dogs. The judge observed all three from different angles before pointing to Maverick. He was chosen as the best of breed from the lineup, and Dan was excited to see him get this honor on the first day. This also meant Maverick would need to be presented in the sporting group with other types of dogs later, so he went back to the benching area to rest Maverick and see if he needed water.

Dan made a few calls to share the good news since there was time before the sporting group judging. Dan wondered if the sporting group order was done the same way as the breed judging. He remembered seeing Maverick in a ring with other types of dogs before, so he assumed this was the same thing. He would find out sooner than expected, as he could now hear the announcement for best of breed winners to return for the sporting group.

Dan led Maverick back to the judging rings and found the sporting group section. He took a place in line with the other handlers and waited for the judge to indicate the start. Soon the judge was pointing and directing the dogs to be walked around the ring, and Dan jogged the perimeter with Maverick when indicated. Then he took Maverick to his place in line behind the other dogs to wait for additional instructions.

The other handlers were taking their dogs around the ring and returning to the line after Dan. Dan was in the middle of the line, so there would be a wait before the judge would evaluate Maverick. The handler behind him started a conversation with him to pass the time. Dan was still nervous, and he wondered if she noticed.

The line moved slowly, but soon enough the judge was evaluating Maverick. When he was finished, the judge directed the handlers to circle the ring with their dogs. The woman Dan had been talking to earlier returned to the line and her dog bumped into Maverick from behind. This caught Maverick off guard and caused him to rear down. Dan helped Maverick to stand back up for judging. Dan assumed it was just an accident or a part of lining up and tried to refocus Maverick on him. The judge instructed the dogs to make their way around the ring again, and Dan ran the perimeter again and returned to the line. The same woman's dog bumped into Maverick again on the second return, causing Maverick to rear down again. Dan looked back at her and her dog before helping Maverick to stand up again. All of the other dogs were standing, so he knew it would look out of place if Maverick was sitting. He tried to get Maverick's attention on him as he waited for the judge's instructions.

The judge pointed to three other dogs to come forward. The three that were chosen won the sporting group in that order, and Maverick did not place. Dan wondered if the sitting had anything to do with it or if he had done something wrong, and he wasn't sure how he could avoid that in the future. Rusty would be there for the next day's judging, and Dan was interested to see how Maverick would do with him in the ring. Maverick would have to win best of breed again to get to the sporting group, though, and Dan didn't want to assume he would make it that far.

Rusty arrived on Friday and took Maverick to the day's Weimaraner judging. Dan made sure to stay away far enough for Maverick to focus, and Rusty returned with the news that Maverick was again selected as best of breed. This was great news for him to get best of breed two days in a row, and that also meant Maverick would return to compete in the sporting group later in the afternoon. Dan wondered how Maverick would do today or if that same dog from yesterday would be behind him. He was sure that if it happened again Rusty would know how to handle it or could at least explain how to avoid it in the future.

Dan explained what had happened the day before to Rusty.

"The dog behind us kept bumping into Maverick causing him to sit down. I was wondering if I wasn't bringing him close enough to the dogs in front of him or just kept stopping in the wrong place, because it happened twice."

"I wouldn't worry about it. We still have today and tomorrow, and I'm sure he'll do fine."

Dan described the handler and the dog, and Rusty said he would try to avoid being near her in the line placement. Rusty agreed to meet Dan after the sporting group judging and made his way to the ring. Dan was far enough away as to not distract Maverick, but he could still see the ring and the dogs. He watched as they waited to enter the ring. After a few minutes the judge motioned for the dogs to enter; they started walking the dogs around the ring. One by one the handlers went around the circumference of the roped ring and stopped in line with the other dogs. Dan noticed that although Rusty had tried to avoid her, the same handler was behind Maverick.

FIFTEEN

Dan saw Rusty follow the same path before coming to a stop behind the other dogs and stacking Maverick by lifting his head and guiding his tail. The same woman came up behind Maverick, and once again her dog bumped Maverick and caused him to rear down. Dan saw Rusty turn toward her and snapped an angry reprimand. The woman moved her dog back, and Rusty returned his attention to Maverick. The judge came around to the dogs and pointed at them for placement. Once again Maverick was not chosen. The remaining dogs were dismissed.

Dan saw Rusty leaving the ring and started walking over to meet him. They met on the edge of the judging rings, and Dan was eager to hear what he had to say.

"Did you see the dog that bumped him? That was the same one from yesterday."

Rusty shook his head. "She was doing that on purpose. Crowding is sometimes expected but bumping is not, and she was intentionally trying to upset Mav. That was a pretty bold move, but I made sure to set her straight."

"So that is what she was doing. I was thinking I did something wrong."

"No," Rusty continued, "you couldn't have done anything to cause that. It was the same dog and the same handler, and today it was definitely intentional. I doubt yesterday's incident was an accident. Often when a competitor sees another dog as a threat, they do this. It's a compliment but also poor sportsmanship."

"Well, I guess I'm a little relieved that it wasn't me. I see he didn't place again, and I wonder if it was because of that."

Rusty agreed, "It's quite possible. We still have one more day to go, and if she's behind me again, she'd be pretty brave to try it again. Let's just hope we don't have to worry about it tomorrow."

"Agreed," Dan said before taking Maverick and heading off for the night.

He felt relieved that he didn't do anything wrong, but at the same time he felt angry that someone would intentionally do that to another dog. It was bad enough watching the wicket issue from the previous show, and he wondered if Maverick would have to constantly face challenges. It was still a miracle he didn't end up in a shelter, neutered or even euthanized, and the battle with his health and weight was not an easy struggle. He made it through all of that and now had to endure unnecessary obstacles such as these. Dan hoped the last day would prove to be an easier one.

Dan met Rusty again the next morning and handed Maverick's lead over.

"Good luck today. Let's hope it's not a repeat of the last two."

"I hope so too, Rusty replied. "See you in a while."

The first round of judging was for the Weimaraner breed. Dan watched the dogs make their usual jog around the ring and line up near the far side. He watched the judge walk the line to the end and slowly back to the front. He stepped back and started pointing to the dogs for them to leave the line and come forward. Maverick was the first one called up, and he stood there with the other two dogs. Dan assumed this was good news and walked over to the far side of the ring to wait for Rusty.

Rusty made his way over with Maverick after a few minutes and confirmed that Maverick was chosen as best of breed once again.

"That's great news. Does this mean he goes into the sporting group again?" Dan asked.

Rusty confirmed, "Yep, back to sporting group again. Let's hope this one is without incident."

"I hope so too," he said as he patted Maverick. "Good luck."

Dan watched them walk away and hoped for the best. Two days in a row there were problems with the sporting group lineup, and a third day would be truly frustrating. Dan moved to another ringside spot to wait and see where the sporting group judging would take place.

After a while he recognized Rusty and saw him leading Maverick to another ring. Dan walked along the roped perimeter until he was in a position to be able to see the dogs and the ring they would be in for judging. The handlers started entering the ring and getting in line. The judge stood at the head of line and evaluated each dog before pointing it around the ring just as on the previous days. The handlers made their way around the ring with the dogs one by one before taking a place in line behind the others. Dan looked behind Rusty and was incredibly relieved to see someone different this time. At least Maverick would finally get a fair chance at being judged without distraction, or so he hoped.

He watched Rusty lead Maverick to the front of the line for the judge's examination. After the judge looked at Maverick, he directed Rusty to follow the others. They made their way around the ring and took their place in line.

Dan was watching the next dog. As the judge directed them around the ring, Dan was waiting to see the line placement and if they came close to Maverick. The handler approached the line and stopped the dog with plenty of room behind Maverick. Dan breathed a sigh of relief and watched as Maverick stood attentively in place.

The remaining handlers made their way around the ring and returned in line. The judge walked up and down the line as he had done before. He stepped backward to the middle of the ring and started pointing at the dogs. Two dogs were directed out of line, and the third was Maverick. Dan wasn't entirely sure which position Maverick was in, but since he was selected from the line he must have placed with the top of the group. He waited until they were finished and walked along the edge of the judging rings to wait for Rusty.

It seemed to be taking longer than usual, so Dan decided to venture down the hallway to see what was going on in other areas. There were still a few obedience courses set up that he noticed as he walked down the corridor. Barking throughout the building echoed off the tall ceilings. He observed a few of the dogs moving from place card to place card obeying commands from their handlers. He walked a little further down and saw a judging ring being disassembled.

He decided to head back to see if Rusty had finished. He made his way to the ringside and saw Rusty and Maverick walking toward him soon after.

"Hey, no bumping today!"

Rusty was smiling. "Yes, it was a nice change. He took third place in the sporting group, and this was his first time doing that. Way to go, Mav," he said as he patted Maverick. Rusty returned his attention to Dan and handed over the lead. "It's pretty exciting to see him still advancing."

"I agree. I was worried after those first two days, but I guess it would still be a great accomplishment no matter what. That, added with the fact that he was chosen as best of breed every day, makes this a success."

Rusty agreed. "He definitely seems to be getting noticed and moving up faster. He looks a lot more refined since we started handling him. Definitely a long road but looking good."

SIXTEEN

The next show was in one week, in Salisbury. Dan found the show while searching online and read about the Weimaraner specialty and sweepstakes that would take place. Puppies and older dogs would be entered by owners paying a fee, and it seemed like something done to lighten the spirit of the competitive part of the show. He read a few comments about the sweepstakes being more about bragging rights and fun, and it seemed interesting. The age requirements excluded Maverick from participating, but Dan was interested to watch it if he had time while there.

The show was hosted by a local Weimaraner club, and in previous years there seemed to be a large number of competitors. Shows of that size usually come with four or five points based on placement. Dan decided he would take Maverick to the show for the Weimaraner specialty. Rusty would not be able to handle Maverick, but Dan figured he would do okay by himself.

Dan had to think about that for a minute. The previous show had been his first time handling Maverick, and it wasn't the greatest experience. Maverick was focused but Dan was nervous, and the bumping in the sporting group didn't help. He figured the bumping was a one-time issue, and he didn't remember seeing it happen at any other shows.

Dan arrived at the Salisbury show with Maverick with time to spare. He looked over the schedule that was sent out earlier in the week and he knew the Weimaraner judging wasn't until the afternoon, so he figured he would have time to walk around and get acquainted with the place and find the location he needed to be at later. He had pre-registered, so that would save some time at the entrance.

Dan was surprised at how big the show was. There were a lot of dogs in varying breeds, ages and sizes everywhere he looked. He stopped at the superintendent's desk to view the information on the sweepstakes. It was just for puppies up to 24 months old and dogs older than seven years old, so it wasn't something he could enter Maverick in while he was there.

Dan made his way to the judging rings as time was approaching for the Weimaraner judging. He searched the signs to find the ring they were assigned to and walked over to prepare to enter with Maverick. After a few minutes, more handlers and Weimaraners appeared. Dan recognized one of the dogs from advertisements he had seen. She was the top female Weimaraner in the country, and the second Weimaraner overall.

Dan started to feel out of his element again. He was among some of the best dogs and handlers in the country and he wasn't a professional handler. He wondered if he would mess up, walk the wrong way, or make Maverick nervous by his own insecurity. He looked around at the perfectly groomed dogs with their experienced and well-known handlers and reflected on his embarrassment the first time in the ring. He had heard many people tell him that anxiety and fear runs down the leash straight to the dog. He looked down to see if Maverick was okay, and the dog looked up reassuringly at Dan as he did once before. *I got this. Stop worrying.* He didn't have much time to ponder further as they were ordered to take their place in the ring.

He led Maverick in and the dog followed with incredible ease. It was as if Maverick knew what to do better than Dan. The handlers lined up their dogs and Dan noticed there was plenty of space between all of the dogs. He breathed a sigh of relief. Maverick didn't seem the least bit fazed but Dan was still nervous.

Maverick ended up being next to the same female Weimaraner Dan had seen earlier, and she was beautiful. Dan refocused on Maverick to prepare to make the rounds around the ring, and soon it was his turn to advance.

He jogged around the ring with Maverick and returned to the line for the judge's inspection. After all the handlers had returned to the line with their dogs, the judge stood back to assess the dogs.

He pointed at the female dog first for the best of breed and next to Maverick as the best of opposite. Dan knew this meant that the female dog was considered the closest to the breed standard, and Maverick was the best Weimaraner of opposite sex to that dog.

He felt a little out of place standing next to such a high-ranked dog, but Maverick still stood as if he knew some show secret Dan hadn't discovered yet. He was surprised how calm and confident Maverick was, and it certainly made his job easier. Maverick placed second both days to the same top female Weimaraner in the country. Dan was happy to have Maverick recognized at what seemed to be an important show with some of the best dogs in the country, and he was glad his nervousness didn't affect the outcome.

Back at home after the show Dan called Rusty to let him know the results. Rusty also informed him that since Maverick's ranking was high enough based on the points he had earned that year, he might be invited to appear at the large annual dog show in New York in February. Even if he wasn't invited, he could still apply to attend. Rusty told him to send in the application and entry fee for Maverick to be able to attend. Dan said that he would, and made plans with Rusty to go to a Raleigh show in March.

Things at the shop were busy, and time seemed to pass faster than Dan realized. He had sent off the application for the big show and was waiting to get the details so he could make arrangements.

A few weeks later, Dan received a letter back stating that Maverick's entry was declined because the show was full. Dan was devastated. He called Rusty and found out that the accepted entries were based on the ones that were sent in first. He was simply late in sending the application. Rusty reassured him there was always next year, but Dan felt that he had let Maverick down. He had worked so hard all year long and had really made such great improvements in his show presence, demeanor, and confidence that it seemed a shame he wouldn't be able to go. Dan vowed to be the first person to send in his application the following year.

The next week was dismal. Dan felt upset and depressed about missing the entry deadline. He spent a good portion of the following days in his office, mostly at his desk with his head in his hands. He knew Maverick didn't know any better, but he couldn't help feeling responsible. Every time he saw Maverick he kept wanting to say he was sorry.

SEVENTEEN

February arrived and instead of thinking about Valentine's Day, Dan noticed the advertisements for the New York show that he had missed. The show started on the 14th and lasted two days. Dan was interested to learn more, but most reports seemed to focus on particular dogs more than on the show details. Monday arrived and Dan made plans to watch the televised coverage to get a feel for what he might see the following year. He didn't know what to expect, but after a few minutes, he was taken aback.

The show location was huge. It was the size of a stadium and looked more like a professional sporting team's championship game than a dog show. He watched the coverage in disbelief. He had been told by many people that this show was extremely important to dog breed fans and represented a year's worth of travel, hard work, and tireless striving for perfection from each dog and handler—but he wasn't expecting this.

There was an electronic ticker between the lower and upper stadium-style seating areas. The large floor was divided into sections with chairs lining the edges. Velvet roping separated the seating area from the judging ring where the dogs were displayed. A spectator was heard explaining how large the arena was and that it was difficult to find her way around.

Dalmatians were being shown in the ring with their handlers. Dan watched as the dogs stood in line with their tails wagging and looking to their handlers for treats. The judge instructed them to make their way around the ring and later inspected each one before they returned to the line. The judge seemed to take his time looking at each dog's teeth, chest and tail and also lifted their legs. Each time the dogs were walked around the ring Dan heard applause from the crowd but couldn't distinguish which ring it was meant for since there were a few sections active at the same time. He watched as the judge chose the top three dogs in the breed and directed them toward the table at the end of the ring. There were three place cards at which they stood; one was for the best of breed, another for best of opposite sex to the first dog, and there was an award of merit placement. The dogs and their handlers posed for pictures with the judge, and the best of breed was the last to leave the ring.

The video cameras switched to what was referred to as the rotunda, and there were numerous dogs on tables getting groomed while people worked around them in tight quarters. He watched as one owner referred to the area as hot and stressful while another explained how he takes his dog to a drive-through for fast food if he wins. The reporter started introducing dogs and explaining their names and stories, and Dan thought there must have been thousands of dogs at the show.

The intimidation lessened when another reporter started listing jobs of the dogs at the show. She explained that although several people think the show is only for the rich and fancy dogs living lives of luxury, several dogs present were working whenever they were not at shows. The areas they worked in ranged from rescue and guide to a diabetic alert dog.

Dan's relief was cut short by the description of another dog competing in the show. The reporter described a poodle that had been flown in by private jet with a team of assistants and a personal veterinarian. Dan felt the most out of his league at that moment than when he had first attended a show.

This show was much more impressive and serious than Dan had originally thought, and he tuned in the next day to watch the Weimaraners compete in the afternoon. If he was able to attend the next year, this would be the group in which Maverick would be seen and judged. He watched the dogs and their handlers follow the same routine as the Dalmatians from the previous day.

Most of them seemed attentive to their handlers, while a few kept looking around. He noticed that the dogs being judged consisted of the same number of males to females. The best of breed chosen was a male, and the female chosen as best of opposite had a familiar name. The dog was bred by the same breeder as Maverick and his dad.

Dan remembered that Maverick's dad had taken best of breed before at this show a few years ago, and he thought Jan must have been very proud to see her dogs doing so well. The show coverage definitely gave him an idea of the scale of show and helped him understand why it was so highly regarded. He hoped they would make it next year, and he had a long year of shows ahead of him.

Within a few weeks Maverick had gained a few pounds and looked stronger than before. Dan also practiced handling Maverick himself and allowing different people to touch him so he wouldn't be startled if a judge evaluated him. Dan remembered watching him run away from the judge in a previous show, so hopefully he would get accustomed to the practice before the next event. He did step back from people the first few times, but after consistent weekly practice he stopped reacting.

Dan found the footage of Maverick's dad winning best of breed in New York a few years before, and he played the video often. He studied the process in the ring and the similarities to other shows. He was most surprised by the almost identical likeness between the two dogs. Maverick's dad had the same contours of the head and facial expression as Maverick, and they could have easily passed for each other. Dan was excited that Maverick might get a chance to go to New York, but there were more shows remaining in the year. The end of March had arrived, and it was time for another show.

Dan headed to Raleigh. He didn't know what to expect since Maverick's first show the previous year wasn't until May. He arrived to find the large commercial-type buildings separated into sections similar to those of other shows. He noticed the blue kennel club banners hung over the red divider sections on the floor between each ring as he passed a smaller breed being judged. He watched as the dogs were led around the ring and eventually up a small ramp for closer inspection by the judge. It was a fairly large show, and he went to find Rusty.

They were able to stay only one day, so this judging would be the only time in the show Maverick would compete. He was chosen as select dog, and shortly afterward Dan prepared to head home. Earning select dog on the first day still awarded points toward

Maverick's grand champion title, so Dan didn't feel too disappointed about leaving. The next show, in Hampton, was Maverick's first last year, and Dan was excited at the thought of going back.

EIGHTEEN

The return to Hampton was bittersweet. Dan remembered how nervous he had been the year before, seeing Maverick in the ring for the first time. It had been his first foray into the world of dog shows. On this anniversary, Dan decided to attend and handle Maverick himself. The previous year Maverick had placed second out of two dogs, but the show had signified his transition from rehabilitated rescue to returning show dog. So much had transpired in the past year including earning a champion title, and now he was working towards a grand champion title.

Walking into the show this year was very different. Although Dan was still nervous about handling Maverick, the place was familiar and didn't seem as daunting this time around. It was the same indoor show he remembered from the year before. The sections were split by dividers for the different breeds; the place was as bright and well-lit as he remembered it, and the indoor canopies were erected in various areas on the concrete floor. Dan was looking for the Weimaraner ring when he noticed a familiar face looking back at him.

"Wow, is that the same dog?"

"Hey Gary, how have you been? Yep, it's Maverick," Dan replied.

Gary had been present for Dan's first meeting with Darlene to discuss handling Maverick in dog shows. He had been there with his dog, just under a year old, seeking the same service. Maverick hadn't looked the greatest at the time considering he was undergoing rehabilitation, was underweight, and was receiving treatment for his infections. Dan remembered feeling embarrassed at the meeting; standing next to Gary and his dog, Dan felt the contrast between healing and healthy dogs was too striking. Now he felt much better seeing Gary again, and he was proud of Maverick's regained health and appearance.

"I swear that's not the same dog. This one looks like a born-and-bred show dog."

They shook hands and turned their attention back to Maverick.

"It's good to see you, and wow what an improvement. I remember when you first got him he looked awful."

"It's been a busy year," Dan said. He explained the issues with Maverick's rehabilitation, the dog show appearances, and the eating issue re-emerging after the anesthesia.

"That sounds like a busy and stressful year, but looking at him now I'd say it was well worth it. How long are you here for?"

"Every day," Dan replied.

"Well, it was great running into you and congrats to you and him on an amazing turnaround. Good luck in the show and hope to see you again soon."

Dan thanked him, wished him luck as well, and turned in the other direction to determine his location and which ring he needed to take Maverick.

He found the Weimaraner judging ring and started to prepare himself for stepping into the ring once again. Maverick seemed indifferent to the noise around him and wagged his tail as they approached the ring. Dan figured he was more nervous than the dog was. He led Maverick to their place in line and went through the judging routine without incident. Maverick was extremely relaxed and obedient, and his demeanor set Dan at ease. The judge must have noticed it as well since Maverick was chosen as best of breed.

Dan was excited about this, but as soon as he thought about the group judging he felt a pang in his stomach. Going to group meant another possibility of the past repeating itself. He was there for the duration of the show and couldn't justify skipping the group judging because of his own fears, so he headed to the information desk to find out where he needed to go next.

Dan led Maverick to the group judging ring and waited to enter until instructed. He took a place in line and looked at the other dogs and handlers around him. There was enough space between each dog and everything seemed fine. He was nervous looking at the professional handlers and seemingly perfect dogs lined up behind him. The judge walked up and down the line of dogs before moving his hands in a sweeping motion for them to start circling the ring.

As Dan looked toward the end of the ring, he noticed a few handlers huddled together in conversation. Cliques were not uncommon in dog shows, but Dan still felt like an outsider being there by himself. As his gaze traveled back toward the front of the line, he noticed a familiar face and smiled.

Darlene was in the sporting group ring with a curly-coated retriever a few spaces down. He broke the line and walked over to her.

"It's nice to see a familiar face here. How have you been?"

She smiled before replying, "Everything's great, how about you? Wow, look at Maverick! He looks great, and here he is in the sporting group. What a change from last year."

They discussed Maverick's progress over the past year. Dan filled Darlene in on the details of previous shows and the tests that had led Maverick to stop eating again. He admitted he was a little nervous to be in the ring with the professional handlers, and he recounted the bumping incident and other underhanded tricks he had witnessed.

"It happens more often than people think," she whispered.

"I'm seeing that more and more. I find myself watching anyone who comes close to him to make sure they don't try anything funny. He doesn't seem to notice, though. He just trots along ring to ring without a care in the world. He's such a different dog. He's happy, carefree, and loves the attention."

Darlene looked at Dan and smiled. "All he needed was the right home."

"So it seems." Dan said he was glad he had run into her and agreed to catch up again soon.

He walked back to his place in line with Maverick and completed the remainder of the group judging. Maverick wasn't chosen to go further in the show that day, so Dan headed home to get some rest before the next day of showing.

Maverick would receive best of breed for the next two days but lacked a placement on the last day. The group showings were not as stressful as the previous one Dan encountered, but he wasn't too worried about placement in that group. Being chosen best of breed added more points towards the grand champion title, and Dan still couldn't believe the difference from the first show to this one.

He was still surprised at Maverick's transformation. He often reflected on his first image of the dog, and to look at him now was remarkable. Maverick was happy, healthy, and had high confidence. Dan thought the larger shows would be intimidating for Maverick, but the larger the show the more excited he became. His performance was better, almost perfect, and this would no doubt improve with the larger upcoming shows.

Next up was Charlottesville, and Rusty would be available to handle Maverick. They had gone the previous year, and Maverick seemed to love these outdoor shows the most. He always seemed more relaxed, showed better, and placed higher. He received his first placement, best of breed, the previous year against nine Weimaraners. Dan was looking forward to returning and eager to see if Maverick placed any differently this year.

NINETEEN

The drive wasn't nearly as long as some of those for previous shows, and Dan was thankful it was only three hours. He handed Maverick off to Rusty as he had done so many times before and waited to hear the results. He found a place along the ring to stand and looked around. He recognized the various rings from last year, and the warm, sunny day felt oddly comfortable. He watched dogs enter and leave the rings for a couple of hours before noticing Rusty walking back with Maverick. Dan walked over to meet them and was eager to hear the results.

"No best of breed this year, but he was chosen as best of opposite sex."

"That's still good, right?" Dan asked.

Rusty nodded. "The dog he was chosen next to is the top female in the country. I'd say it's an honor. It's the same female he took opposite to at the specialty in Salisbury."

"Some pretty fierce competition this year, it sounds. I'm glad we came, and he still gets points toward grand for best of opposite, right?"

"Sure does. Hopefully we'll see the same or better for tomorrow. He makes it pretty effortless and is showing better every time."

The next day wouldn't bring disappointment. The same female took best of breed, and Maverick was chosen once again to stand next to her as the best of opposite. Dan was excited for Maverick, but he knew from the previous year that more shows were coming up.

The Weimaraner national show was next, so Dan made plans to have Maverick there. They hadn't attended this show the previous year, so he wasn't sure what to expect. Local or regional kennel clubs would sponsor the show, and the location was subject to change. This year it was in Wilmington, a city that listed the creation of the banana split as its claim to fame. Dan laughed upon learning this fact and knew Maverick would be pleased if ice cream was involved.

The Ohio show was indoors at a large convention center. Dan was staying at one of the nearby hotels and made his way to the center for the conformation rounds. This large show usually had more than 100 dogs—all Weimaraners—and the week-long schedule included many other areas of judging. There were agility trials, hunting and tracking tests, rating tests, sweepstakes, seminars on breeding education, breed-specific genetic information, and a banquet before the specialty judging reached a conclusion. It was a very busy schedule all involving Weimaraners, and Dan felt intimidated by the size of the event.

Dan made his way indoors and found the room for conformation judging. He walked in and noted the large room, which looked to be the length of a football field compared to previous shows. The judging ring made up the center and largely dominated the room. It was partitioned off by white plastic chains connected by white metal stands. Green carpeting was rolled along the inside perimeter of the chained ring and diagonally across the floor. He saw some dogs lined up in the corners and others making their way around the ring with their handlers. Grey metal chairs with fabric backs and seat covers lined the outside of the ring with more scattered against the walls. The ceiling was tall and lined with rows of multiple drop lights and an occasional chandelier. The room was brightly lit and the tall ceilings reverberated the barks back into the room with an echo.

Dan walked to the entrance of the ring and noticed pens erected against the walls. Most of them included sleeping dogs, which he assumed had already been shown or grew tired of waiting to enter the ring. He walked to the other wall and turned to find Rusty. He handed over Maverick's lead and asked, "This is a big place, huh?"

"This is nationals; nothing but Weims."

"So I see. Good luck, buddy," he said as he patted Maverick.

He walked away and found a spot to stand to watch the activity. A little while had passed before he saw Rusty and Maverick inside the roped ring. He watched as they went through the regular routine of running the ring, being judged in line, inspected individually and back around again. There was a table near the opening of the ring that displayed ribbons and certificates. He saw the dogs make their way to the exit and noticed that a few stayed behind in front of the table. Maverick was included in the remaining dogs, and Dan would later learn that he had made the first cut. Dan considered it an honor that Maverick was chosen out of so many other dogs. This was an all-Weimaraner show, after all, and some of the best dogs in the country were in attendance.

The next day followed the same routine, and once again Maverick made the first cut. He did not advance in the second round, but Dan was happy he placed so well in such stiff competition. The next show would have Maverick back in Canfield. Dan wouldn't be able to attend because of work, but Maverick was able to stay with Rusty until the show.

The previous year's show almost didn't happen. Dan remembered the hives all over Maverick's back just weeks before the show and waking up several times during the night to check on him. The miraculous clearing just two days before they had to leave was a huge relief. That was also his first five-point major, so Dan was anxiously awaiting Rusty's call to see how he fared this year.

The weather was warm for the outdoor show in August, and Rusty called with the news that Maverick had been chosen as select dog every day. By the end of the three days, Maverick had earned enough points to be considered a grand champion. Dan was extremely excited to hear this news, and Rusty promised to send him pictures soon before heading back to bring Maverick home.

TWENTY

A few weeks later Dan was checking the mail and received a welcome surprise; an invitation to the Eukanuba National Championship. He called Rusty immediately, only to find out that earning the grand champion designation at Canfield meant Maverick was guaranteed an invite. Rusty explained that any dog receiving a grand champion designation during a certain period that year would be invited. Dogs were also eligible if they had won best of breed at a specialty show or a best in show at an all breed show. Dan still thought it was pretty cool that Maverick was getting invites to bigger shows, and from what Rusty explained, going to Eukanuba was certainly an honor.

The show was in California the previous year, and Dan was relieved to find out it would be held in Florida. He wouldn't be able to make a California trip, but he figured he could make the 15-hour drive to Florida without much trouble. Since Maverick had already achieved his grand champion title, Dan decided to take a few months off until it was time to head to the Eukanuba show. Everything seemed to be falling in place, and he made plans to meet Rusty in Florida later in the year.

Dan got a call before the show from Eukanuba. They had heard one of the dogs coming to the show was a rescue and wanted to know more about the story. Dan explained how he came to own Maverick and the ride he was taken on since acquiring him that brought him into the world of dog shows. He agreed to meet with them at the show to discuss the story more and possibly do an interview. Dan was happy someone was interested in Maverick's story, but he didn't know what to expect. He wasn't used to doing interviews and was already nervous at the idea of heading to such a prestigious show. It wouldn't do him much good to worry about it, and he figured the Florida trip was going to be exciting.

The 15-hour drive was quick and uneventful with Maverick leisurely enjoying the scenery between naps, a stop for fuel and a few breaks for exercise. Dan arrived the night before the show to allow enough time to check into the hotel, get settled, and take Maverick out for some additional exercise after being in the truck most of the day.

They got an early start the next morning and drove over to the center. Dan was nervous heading in for the day. He looked up the convention center the night before and found out that it was a huge facility covering over 2 million square feet and containing so many retail stores and food courts it sounded like it housed a shopping mall inside. He looked over the floor plans and directions on the website to get an idea of where he needed to go to get started.

They weren't able to go straight to the building. Large buses were stationed at the parking lot to shuttle participants to the center. Upon arrival he learned some buses were only for people and others were designated for people and dogs. The bus accepting dogs was already gone, so he had to wait for another bus to return.

As he walked along the parking lot he passed another bus; the driver called him over and asked about Maverick.

"That's a fine looking dog you have there. Is he in the show today?"

"Yes sir," Dan replied, "he's all ready to go."

The driver walked up the steps and looked down the aisle of the interior of the bus before coming back to Dan.

"I have two seats left. I'm not supposed to take dogs, but you might be waiting a while. I assume he's trained and won't be trouble?"

"He's used to riding and will be fine."

"Come on in, then," he said as he waived Dan aboard the bus.

Dan found the remaining two seats and allowed Maverick to jump up and sit on the one by the window. The dog immediately attracted the attention of the other riders, and soon people were taking photos and asking questions about Maverick. They were petting him and treating him like a celebrity, and Dan watched and laughed as Maverick was happy to perform for his newfound fans. He was able to get a few pictures of Maverick for himself before they arrived at the center.

He thanked the driver for letting them tag along and walked toward the main entrance. Upon walking in he immediately noticed the welcome banner hanging up high. A Weimaraner was featured on the banner, and Dan figured that had to be as good a sign as any that it was going to be a good day.

He navigated the large facility and tried to find Rusty. It was a long, rectangular building, and Dan didn't know if he should head left or right to start looking. Before he could decide, his phone rang. The call was from Laura, the woman he was supposed to meet for the interview about Maverick. She was delighted that he was already on the premises and gave him directions to her location in the center. He headed in that direction with Maverick and would look for Rusty afterward.

It was one hour before the start of the show, and Maverick was groomed and ready. Eukanuba had a booth set up in between the traffic of people and dogs navigating throughout the hall. They met Laura, who discussed some of the questions they would cover. She was very friendly and appeared genuinely interested in Maverick's history. She listened as Dan briefly covered some key points in their journey, and she played with Maverick until it was time to start recording.

The cameras started recording, and Dan introduced himself and Maverick. He explained his Weimaraner rescue and its location and revealed the story behind him acquiring Maverick. He discussed wanting to get him back to a proper weight and allow him to return to the show ring since that is what he was bred to do.

She asked about his training and nutrition. She knew that Dan was a positive reinforcement trainer and that nutrition played a large role in any dog's rehabilitation. Dan explained the eating issues with Maverick and the many foods they had tried before mixing Eukanuba's active and puppy brands together to put the weight back on him. Dan described the changes in his eating habits and how well he was now doing with his food drive. Maverick had regained a normal food and energy drive and was as healthy and energetic as any other Weimaraner his age should be.

The next question she asked was about Maverick's home life outside the show ring. Dan described the other Weimaraners he had at home and at the shop, as well as Gracie, who keeps Maverick in line as his girlfriend. Laura smiled at the camera and said, "Listen up, bitches, he's taken!"

Dan laughed and they continued the interview. She asked what his expectations were for the show, and Dan revealed that he was happy with any outcome as long as Maverick's tail was wagging and he was happy. He explained that Maverick loves to show and that it was what he was bred to do. She wrapped up the interview and asked if Maverick had any last words. He was looking at the excitement going on around him and focused on Dan when Laura asked to see one of his signature hugs. Dan placed his hands on his chest and Maverick promptly jumped up with both paws. Laura closed the interview, then grabbed his paws and got a hug of her own.

Dan thanked her for the interview and set out to find Rusty to tell him about their time in front of the cameras. Judging was about to start, and he had made it back with just a few minutes to spare.

TWENTY-ONE

Dan handed Maverick's lead to Rusty and told him he had received a confirmation letter from Westminster.

"Already?" Rusty was surprised.

"Yes. I wasn't waiting like last year. I sent off the paperwork as soon as possible and got the confirmation just before this show. We're going to New York."

"That's incredible. To think how Maverick started out, and to end up in New York is amazing," Rusty said.

"Trust me, it's hard for me to take all this in too. I never would have thought he'd take me on such a wild ride. Talk about a great way to end the year."

"No kidding." The announcement for Weimaraners was made, and it was time for Rusty to take Maverick into the ring. "Back in a bit."

Dan watched Rusty and Maverick head into the ring for judging. This show was decorated in a more elegant manner than other shows. The rich blue carpeting was enclosed with red velvet ropes, and he watched as Maverick took a place in line. As the dogs made their way around the ring and were inspected individually, Dan recognized two of the dogs as the top male Weimaraners in the country. Both looked perfect as they stood near-motionless while being evaluated.

The dogs returned to the line, and the judge walked back and forth analyzing them for advancement. He started pointing to the dogs to walk toward the end of the ring for additional judging, and Dan wasn't surprised when he saw the two males he recognized earlier get chosen and move to the other side. He was, however, very surprised to see Maverick following them and being chosen for the first cut.

Maverick was stacked behind the same two males and looked just as handsome as they did. They were evaluated again and chosen for placement, and Maverick was dismissed. Dan walked over to meet Rusty as the ring cleared out.

"Standing right behind the top two males—not bad, eh?" he asked Rusty.

"Not bad at all. In fact, that was the best he ever showed, in my opinion. To get chosen for the first cut considering the other dogs he was with, that's definitely impressive. He's so good at this now he could probably show himself," Rusty joked.

"Not so fast," Dan laughed. "We're going to need you for New York."

"Looking forward to it," Rusty replied.

Dan took Maverick back to the hotel to gather their things and start the 15-hour drive home. He was pleased Maverick did so well, and the focus would be turning solely on the upcoming New York show. Dan recalled watching the show on television and still felt intimidated, but the excitement was doing a good job of masking his slight fear. He was relieved that they would be able to go this year, especially considering that last year they had missed out only because of a late application.

Back home things quickly returned to the usual routine, with the momentum of the New York show slowly building in the background. Dan received an email from the show with a questionnaire. It asked questions about the dog, show experience, and history, which Dan jokingly completed with a note explaining that Maverick was the one responsible for getting him into this. The form also asked for contact information in case the media wanted to contact him. He filled out the information without hesitation and was planning to write a summary of Maverick's story. A friend who had seen the video from Eukanuba suggested that Dan contact one of the animal media channels about Maverick and send in a summary about his transformation. He only had time to send it to one media outlet and forgot about it.

February was getting closer and excitement was building about the show. The clients who had originally told Dan about Maverick's listing stopped by the shop to take pictures with the dog and wish him luck. Dan started getting calls from people who had read about Maverick's story; it seemed the media outlet Dan had sent the summary to ended up publishing it a week before the show. Calls came from all over: Australia, New Zealand, Canada, and even one from England.

One of the calls was from a writer at Pets Adviser who conducted an interview over the phone. The interview and the story appeared two days before the show, and Eukanuba had also contacted him. They wanted to interview Dan with Maverick in New York before the competition and use Maverick in some of their advertisements. Dan was surprised about the interest people were taking in Maverick's story, and he was willing to do the interviews. He made arrangements for the interview and started packing for the trip.

Monday morning Dan left with Maverick to make the drive to New York. The drive was uneventful and they arrived in the late afternoon. Driving into the city he noticed the Empire State Building was lit up at the top with purple and gold lights in honor of the show. It was already getting dark and he needed to find the hotel.

Hotel Pennsylvania was across the street from where the show would take place. Dan found it easily by recognizing the marquee and parked before heading in to the lobby. Soon after he and Maverick entered the lobby people started coming up to Dan and asking questions. They asked to pet Maverick and if he would be in the show tomorrow. Some of them took photographs and wished him good luck. Dan figured it must have looked odd to walk into a hotel with a large grey dog, but Maverick was enjoying all the attention.

After the spectators left he checked in and asked for a room with a view of the Empire State Building. The staff was happy to oblige, and Dan headed to the room to unpack and take photographs of the building. One of the items he unpacked was incredibly special and unique. Dan's friends from Ohio had made a custom coat for Maverick in case it was cold in New York. It was a fleece-lined waterproof coat with his name and title embroidered on the outside. Dan wasn't sure if they would get to use it since it seemed pretty warm outside.

Dan took Maverick downstairs to go for a walk. He exited the lobby and walked around looking for grass, but all he could find was concrete. There didn't seem to be any ground suitable for dogs to relieve themselves, and he settled on the dirt around one of the trees on the sidewalk. He headed back to the room and checked over Maverick as he settled down. He seemed cool and fine without reason to worry. Dan called the person from Eukanuba who would be doing the interview, and they agreed to meet in the lobby early the next morning. He didn't have to be checked in at the show until late morning, so there was plenty of time for the interview and to walk Maverick again.

Dan settled in for the night and turned on the television. The show was being broadcast, and he felt odd watching it knowing it was going on right across the street. He watched it for a little while before checking on Maverick again. The dog seemed clueless and happy lying there wagging his tail. Dan was excited about the next day but figured it would be best to get some sleep.

TWENTY-TWO

Tuesday morning started with a walk for Maverick and a light breakfast. Dan met with the Eukanuba representative, who turned out to be a veterinarian. She joked that no one could ever pronounce her last name correctly, and calling her Jessica or Dr. V would work. She asked questions about Maverick, Dan, the show, and what led up to them being in New York. Dan explained the story of being alerted to the listing for Maverick, detailed his injuries and recovery, and went over a brief summary of the shows that led him to New York. She wanted to take some pictures of him and Maverick, but the lighting was dim. They walked to other corners of the lobby looking for a suitable area, and they found a corner with benches along the wall that seemed well lit. There were a few people around and dogs were coming and going through the lobby, but a small crowd had formed near Maverick. People were taking their own pictures and asking about him, and Dan stopped to talk to them. Before he could return to Jessica and continue the interview, more people approached to ask about Maverick. Dan apologized to her, but she was just as surprised to see so many people drawn to the dog. She expressed a desire to write a separate story about Maverick, and Dan appreciated her interest.

They wrapped up the interview and Dan promised to get her pictures of Maverick after the show. He went back to the hotel room to get a few things before heading across the street. One thing he was sure not to forget was the paperwork. He was sternly warned that without all required documentation, especially the release form, he would not be able to enter the facility or be allowed to leave if already inside. He checked the papers again to make sure he had everything and left the room to head to the show.

He walked into the building with Maverick and tried to call Rusty. There was no answer, so he walked around to look for him. There were people everywhere. He had read that the show was expecting an estimated 2,000 dogs, and it looked like they were all here judging by how packed the crating area appeared. Dan ran into Rusty's assistant, and she explained that he was by one of the booths. Dan thanked her and headed in that direction, but when he got there he saw a long line of booths and no sign of Rusty. He grabbed his phone to try to call Rusty again, but before he could dial, his phone rang.

The caller identified himself as a producer from ABC News and asked to meet Dan inside the building. They decided on a meeting location and Dan went to the entrance to the benching area to wait. People stopped to ask questions and were taking pictures of Maverick. The only dogs allowed in the show were dogs that were competing, so the questions were different from those of the spectators in the hotel lobby. People knew that if a dog was seen inside the building at this show, the dog was competing.

One man walked up to Dan and took pictures of Maverick. He explained that he was writing a book about dogs at the show and asked Dan to sign a release for his name and Maverick's photograph to be used. Dan finished signing the form just as the ABC News producer appeared. He asked questions about Maverick, his handler, and verified some information from the articles. He asked if they could do an interview on camera since their reporter was on his way to the show. Dan agreed and the producer put in a call to arrange the interview. There was still no sign of Rusty. It was an incredibly large venue packed with people and dogs, but Dan knew they would make contact eventually. He noticed Maverick getting tired, so he headed to the crating area. The producer followed Dan to the crating area, and Rusty was there as well. Around the same time, the reporter, also named Dan, showed up and was introduced to Dan and Maverick. They looked around for a suitable place to film the interview and found a nearby hall. Before they could even set up, they were noticed by security and sent back inside. They found a small open area in the back of a room and decided to film the interview there.

The reporter discussed the story with Dan and revealed he's really a cat person, but he was comfortable around Maverick and was even petting him. He asked Dan what he would do if he won, and Dan was overcome with emotion as he struggled to find a reply. He explained that he hadn't really thought about it and was just proud that Maverick had come so far. Just being at the show was incredibly unexpected, and he felt lucky to have found Maverick and been taken as far as he was. People walking by stopped and asked if the dog had won, to which the two Dans chuckled and replied that judging for his breed had not yet started.

They finished the interview and Dan took Maverick back to his crate, where he sat inside. The dogs usually have to be contained at shows when they are not being groomed or judged, and Maverick didn't have any issues with this short-term confinement.

Dan asked the reporter which local station would broadcast the interview, and he was surprised when he was told it would appear on the network's world news report with Diane Sawyer. Dan was shocked but really had no time to let it sink in. He needed to talk to Rusty and get ready for the judging.

Dan and Rusty talked for about half an hour until it was time for Rusty to get Maverick ready to enter the ring. Dan went to sit in the stands to watch, and he was surprised to find Dan from ABC and the cameraman joining him. Dan explained to the reporter what to expect and what would happen when judging started. The call was made for Weimaraners, and soon they could see Rusty and Maverick on the green carpet. Rusty led Maverick to a place in line third from the front. Dan watched as the dogs started running the perimeter of the ring, and a realization hit him. Here was a previously skinny, neglected, and unwanted dog transformed and running around the New York show while a news crew sat alongside him and recorded every minute. The reporter asked what would happen if Maverick won.

"I don't know, but this is far beyond anything I ever expected," Dan replied. "I always watched this show on television but never imagined I would be here, and especially not showing a dog that looked as bad as some of our other rescues. It's all so unexpected and overwhelming."

Dan took pictures as the dogs went through their typical routine and inspections. Maverick's tail was up and he looked happy. Despite his rough beginning, the dog looked to Dan like he belonged in the ring next to the other dogs. The reporter asked if Dan was nervous, but he replied that he was just happy to be at the show. The judge started pulling dogs from the line to designate the winners, and Dan noticed the first dog pulled was the top female Weimaraner in the country. She won the best of breed. Best opposite went to the top male Weimaraner, who had won best of breed the year before at the same show. The final placement was chosen for the award of merit, and the dogs were dismissed. Dan watched Rusty lead Maverick out of the ring and explained to the reporter that he was going to meet them.

TWENTY–THREE

Dan caught up with Rusty, followed by the news crew. Rusty and Dan agreed that Maverick showed very well and that the chosen winners were well-deserving. The news crew took some more video footage and asked if Dan was disappointed. Maverick jumped up to give Dan one of his signature hugs and Dan replied, "This is what it's all about. This is what it's all about every day."

The reporter reached over to pet Maverick before Dan let him down and took him to his crate. He must have been exhausted given how fast he curled up and went to sleep. Dan finished up with the news crew and was told the story would air later that evening. Security would not let anyone leave the building until a specific time, and even though they changed it to an hour earlier, Dan would still miss the broadcast. He called his parents and asked them to record it for him. They agreed and called a few other family members to make sure it would be covered.

The time arrived for the segment to air on television, and shortly afterward Dan's phone was ringing. The shop was still open and someone there called to let him know they were being inundated with calls about Maverick from clients who had seen the news report. Dan's phone continued to ring and chirp with notifications from emails and text messages. He couldn't answer them fast enough with everything going on around him, and people were still coming up to him to ask about his dog.

One of the people who came to talk to Dan was a handler who had shown Maverick as a puppy. She was there showing her own dog and hadn't seen Maverick in four years. She explained her disappointment with his prior treatment and was delighted Dan had found him. She was excited to see him again and thanked Dan for what he had done. Other people were still approaching; some wanted to look at the dog, while others asked questions. A few people had heard about his Weimaraner rescue and offered compliments on his efforts.

As the people left and Dan's phone finally stopped chirping with notifications, he noticed it was time to leave. He woke up Maverick and gathered their things to head back to the hotel and get something to eat. After dinner he checked his email and couldn't believe how many he had waiting. Many were from people he didn't know, and he went through them and replied to a few before hanging out with Maverick and watching the rest of the show on television. They hadn't gotten to the best in show judging yet, but Dan fell asleep with Maverick while waiting.

The next morning he checked online and found out which dog had won best in show. Dan received a few more calls and emails, one of which was from the ABC affiliate in his hometown. He replied to a few before packing up for the drive home. The drive was uneventful, and Dan felt wiped out from the excitement and the trip.

Stories started appearing on different websites, some of which had not contacted Dan. He assumed they had read some of the other articles or saw the interview on the news. The show officials contacted Dan to get approval to post his story on two social media pages, and he agreed. He started keeping a list of links to all the stories and videos about Maverick and the show. He found the Eukanuba interview online and laughed when he noticed they had edited out the reporter's reference to Maverick having a girlfriend. He looked through some of the social media reports and couldn't believe how many people were responding. Judges, ring stewards, and even celebrity handlers had commented on Maverick's story.

Friends and clients at the shop commented about stories they had read or seen about Maverick, and one noticed a Eukanuba advertisement featuring Maverick in a national magazine for outdoor enthusiasts. Another client messaged Dan a week later upon seeing another advertisement featuring Maverick in a dog magazine. Dan didn't even know about some of these appearances, and he wondered where else Maverick's story was featured. He contacted one of the Eukanuba representatives and learned of another ad that would appear in the main kennel club's handbook. The advertisement would feature Maverick's story and be given to every person who registered a dog with the club.

Dan was continuously surprised by the outpouring of support and interest, and laughed when someone asked him about a book or movie. There were many details most of the news stories hadn't covered, and he would love the chance to share the entire story. Perhaps in time he would have that opportunity. Until then, he decided that Maverick, Grand Champion Anson's Unforgettable, would choose for himself what he wanted to do next. Dock diving, agility, competitive obedience, hunting tests—these were just a few of the possibilities for this incredible boy. Perhaps he will take Dan on another unforgettable journey.

About the Author
Dan Stallings

Dan Stallings spent 17 years in healthcare and had a successful career before deciding to do what he really loved – being with his dogs. He went to school and became a certified dog trainer. Shortly thereafter he opened his own dog daycare, boarding, grooming and training facility in Virginia Beach, Virginia. His business quickly grew as people saw his love and passion for dogs was evident.

He realized shortly after opening that he had the space and desire to help not only the dogs of his clients, but also less fortunate dogs. This led him to found Mid-Atlantic Weimaraner Rescue. It's anything but a shelter; the rescued Weimaraners spend their days lounging on sofas, running around a lush grass field, swimming in saltwater pools and getting plenty of social interaction with people and other dogs. He also ensures they receive the very best nutrition and veterinary care. Many of these Weimaraners have never known love, compassion or any quality of life prior to coming to his facility.

Upon learning he was also a trainer, many other rescue groups began seeking him out to help with their difficult rescues whose only other option was euthanasia. Before he realized it, Dan's rescue was a lot bigger than he had ever imagined. He also adopts the most unadoptable dogs with the worst behavior issues or the ones who have previously suffered the most, rehabilitating them over months and even years before finding a suitable 'job' for them (which they often pick themselves).

Dan has taken some of his own rescues he's trained and won dock diving events, competitive obedience trials and now conformation events. If you ask him, he'll proudly tell you he does it to show everyone: "It's not the dog. It never was. It was the owners who didn't understand or care enough to spend time with their dogs and find something to do with them that they both could enjoy. Look what I've gotten in return."

About the Author
K.B. Lacoste

K.B. Lacoste is an author, poet and pet lover from Louisiana. A self-professed workaholic, she tries to balance her quest for a Ph.D. with work, travel, writing about pets and visiting her local shelter as often as possible. Her love for writing and animals started at a young age with cats, dogs and many frogs.

To find out what Maverick, Dan and the rest of the crew are up to now, visit:

Website:
www.oneunforgettablejourney.com

Facebook: www.facebook.com/MavericksJourney

Twitter:
@MavsJourney

Thee Dog House:
www.facebook.com/theedoghouse

23459955R00084

Made in the USA
Middletown, DE
27 August 2015